THE
SCIENCE FICTION
& FANTASY
QUIZ BOOK

THE
SCIENCE FICTION
& FANTASY
QUIZ BOOK

Joseph A. McCullough

First published in Great Britain in 2015 by Osprey Publishing
This revised edition first published in 2017
PO Box 883, Oxford, OX1 9PL, UK
1385 Broadway, 5th Floor, New York, NY 10018, USA
Email: info@ospreypublishing.com

Osprey Publishing, part of Bloomsbury Publishing Plc

A CIP catalog record for this book is available from the British Library

Joseph A. McCullough has asserted his right under the Copyright, Designs and Patents Act, 1988,
to be identified as the Author of this Work.

ISBN: 978 1 4728 2904 7
ePub ISBN: 978 1 4728 1085 4
PDF ISBN: 978 1 4728 1084 7

Typeset in Adobe Garamond Pro and Trade Gothic
Printed in China through World Print Ltd.

17 18 19 20 21   10 9 8 7 6 5 4 3 2 1

Osprey Publishing supports the Woodland Trust, the UK's leading woodland conservation charity.
Between 2014 and 2018 our donations will be spent on their Centenary Woods project in the UK.

www.ospreypublishing.com

DEDICATION

With special thanks to Steph and Freya McCullough,
Karen McCullough, Phil Smith, Laura Callaghan,
and Sam Downes.

QUIZZES

DIFFICULTY LEVEL: EASY

QUIZ 1
GENERAL KNOWLEDGE, MULTIPLE CHOICE

1. Who directed the 1986 film *Aliens*?
   - ☐ a) Paul Verhoeven
   - ☐ b) James Cameron
   - ☐ c) John Carpenter
   - ☐ d) Steven Spielberg

2. Stan Lee served as both the president and chairman of which of these comic book companies?
   - ☐ a) Marvel
   - ☐ b) DC
   - ☐ c) Image
   - ☐ d) Dynamite

3. Which science-fiction television series featured aliens called Goa'uld?
   - ☐ a) *Star Trek: The Next Generation*
   - ☐ b) *The X-Files*
   - ☐ c) *Stargate: SG-1*
   - ☐ d) *Battlestar Galactica*

4. What is the title of the second book in the Harry Potter series?
   - ☐ a) *Harry Potter and the Prisoner of Azkaban*
   - ☐ b) *Harry Potter and the Goblet of Fire*
   - ☐ c) *Harry Potter and the Chamber of Secrets*
   - ☐ d) *Harry Potter and the Philosopher's Stone*

5. Who portrayed the character Willow Rosenberg in the television series *Buffy the Vampire Slayer*?
   - ☐ a) Charisma Carpenter
   - ☐ b) Michelle Trachtenberg
   - ☐ c) Kristine Sutherland
   - ☐ d) Alyson Hannigan

6. What is *Zork*?

☐ a) a comic book

☐ b) a novel

☐ c) a computer game

☐ d) a radio show

7. Which television show featured a character nicknamed "Starbuck"?

☐ a) *Buck Rogers*

☐ b) *Battlestar Galactica*

☐ c) *Space: Above and Beyond*

☐ d) *Stargate: SG-1*

8. What was the title of the second Conan movie to feature Arnold Schwarzenegger?

☐ a) *Conan the Destroyer*

☐ b) *Conan the Conqueror*

☐ c) *Conan the Usurper*

☐ d) *Conan the Warrior*

9. In the *Star Wars* universe, what species is Chewbacca?

☐ a) Jawa

☐ b) Trandoshan

☐ c) Ewok

☐ d) Wookiee

10. Which character does Scarlett Johansson play in the 2012 film *The Avengers*?

☐ a) Wasp

☐ b) Black Widow

☐ c) Silver Sable

☐ d) Scarlet Witch

QUIZ 2

GENERAL KNOWLEDGE, MULTIPLE CHOICE

1. In *The X-Files*, what is Agent Scully's first name?
   - ☐ a) Alice
   - ☐ b) Jean
   - ☐ c) Dana
   - ☐ d) Linda

2. Which character did Liam Neeson play in *Star Wars: Episode I – The Phantom Menace*?
   - ☐ a) Qui-Gon Jinn
   - ☐ b) Obi-Wan Kenobi
   - ☐ c) Anakin Skywalker
   - ☐ d) Nute Gunray

3. Who wrote the novel *The Time Machine*, first published in 1895?
   - ☐ a) Edward Page Mitchell
   - ☐ b) Jules Verne
   - ☐ c) H. G. Wells
   - ☐ d) Edward Bellamy

4. Which of these was a recurring villain in *Star Trek: The Next Generation*?
   - ☐ a) B
   - ☐ b) F
   - ☐ c) L
   - ☐ d) Q

5. Which of these Dwarves was NOT a member of Thorin Oakenshield's company in J. R. R. Tolkien's novel *The Hobbit*?
   - ☐ a) Ori
   - ☐ b) Gimli
   - ☐ c) Dwalin
   - ☐ d) Bifur

6. Master Chief is the protagonist of which science-fiction video game?

☐ a) *Halo*

☐ b) *Mass Effect*

☐ c) *Gears of War*

☐ d) *Doom*

7. *Torchwood* is a spin-off from which science-fiction television series?

☐ a) *Blake's 7*

☐ b) *Doctor Who*

☐ c) *Stargate: SG-1*

☐ d) *Lost*

8. Which character from *The Princess Bride* is a giant?

☐ a) Vizzini

☐ b) Fezzik

☐ c) Westley

☐ d) Miracle Max

9. The Minotaur was the son of a woman and which animal?

☐ a) a horse

☐ b) a lion

☐ c) a bull

☐ d) a snake

10. Who directed the 1982 film *Blade Runner*?

☐ a) Steven Spielberg

☐ b) James Cameron

☐ c) Ridley Scott

☐ d) George Lucas

QUIZ 3
GENERAL KNOWLEDGE, TRUE OR FALSE

1. Katniss Everdeen represented District 9 at the Hunger Games.
    ☐ True   ☐ False

2. Wonder Woman is actually an Amazon princess.
    ☐ True   ☐ False

3. In *The Lord of the Rings*, Pippin's full name is Peter Todd Took.
    ☐ True   ☐ False

4. Severus Snape is Harry Potter's second cousin.
    ☐ True   ☐ False

5. *A Song of Ice and Fire* is the official name of George R. R. Martin's series of books that begins with *A Game of Thrones*.
    ☐ True   ☐ False

6. Barsoom was Edgar Rice Burroughs' invented name for the planet Venus.
    ☐ True   ☐ False

7. Vulcan blood is blue when exposed to oxygen.
    ☐ True   ☐ False

8. Bram Stoker's *Dracula* was the first vampire novel.
    ☐ True   ☐ False

9. *The Hobbit* was first published in French.
    ☐ True   ☐ False

10. Scientology was founded by science-fiction writer L. Ron Hubbard.
    ☐ True   ☐ False

QUIZ 4
GENERAL KNOWLEDGE QUESTIONS, SHORT ANSWER

1. According to *Return of the Jedi*, on what planet does Jabba the Hutt live?

....

2. What 1992 science-fiction sequel features the subtitle "Judgment Day"?

....

3. Complete this phrase as it relates to Spider-Man: "With great power…"

....

4. Who is "The Once and Future King"?

....

5. What novel served as the basis for the 1982 film *Blade Runner*?

....

6. Which character was played by Mark Ruffalo in the 2012 film *The Avengers*?

....

7. Close encounters of the *which* kind?

....

8. What kind of creature will you become if you catch lycanthropy?

....

9. What is the code name of X-Men founder Charles Xavier?

....

10. Which term came first, "cyberpunk" or "steampunk"?

....

QUIZ 5
SPACESHIPS, MATCH UP

Match up these science-fiction heroes with their spaceships.

1. Malcolm Reynolds

2. Han Solo

3. The Doctor

4. William Adama

5. Kathryn Janeway

6. Juzo Okita

7. Dylan Hunt

8. Buck Rogers

9. John Sheridan

10. James T. Kirk

a) Battlestar *Galactica*

b) USS *Enterprise*

c) TARDIS

d) *Ranger 3*

e) *Serenity*

f) *Andromeda Ascendant*

g) *White Star*

h) *Space Battleship Yamato*

i) *Millennium Falcon*

j) USS *Voyager*

QUIZ 6
GENERAL KNOWLEDGE, MULTIPLE CHOICE

1. Who was the third actor to portray the title role in *Doctor Who* on television?
   - ☐ a) Jon Pertwee
   - ☐ b) Tom Baker
   - ☐ c) Patrick Troughton
   - ☐ d) Peter Davidson

2. Which 2005 film continued the story of the short-lived television show *Firefly*?
   - ☐ a) *Serenity*
   - ☐ b) *Splicer*
   - ☐ c) *Silent Running*
   - ☐ d) *City of Lost Children*

3. In C. S. Lewis's *The Lion, the Witch and the Wardrobe*, what type of creature is Mr Tumnus?
   - ☐ a) Centaur
   - ☐ b) Satyr
   - ☐ c) Faun
   - ☐ d) Glaistig

4. In which year was *Star Wars: A New Hope* first released in the United States?
   - ☐ a) 1975
   - ☐ b) 1977
   - ☐ c) 1979
   - ☐ d) 1981

5. Which alien species is most likely to wield a bat'leth?
   - ☐ a) Vulcan
   - ☐ b) Romulan
   - ☐ c) Klingon
   - ☐ d) Borg

6. How many claws does Marvel Comics' Wolverine possess?
   - ☐ a) 2
   - ☐ b) 4
   - ☐ c) 6
   - ☐ d) 8

7. Who wrote the novel *The Wonderful Wizard of Oz*?
   - ☐ a) John R. Neill
   - ☐ b) Ruth Plumly Thompson
   - ☐ c) P. T. Barnum
   - ☐ d) L. Frank Baum

8. Which type of creature does Anita Blake normally hunt?
   - ☐ a) Vampires
   - ☐ b) Werewolves
   - ☐ c) Ghosts
   - ☐ d) Demons

9. Who plays Tyrion Lannister in the television series *Game of Thrones*?
   - ☐ a) Iwan Rheon
   - ☐ b) Richard Madden
   - ☐ c) Sean Bean
   - ☐ d) Peter Dinklage

10. In *The Hobbit*, the character of Beorn can change into which animal?
    - ☐ a) a lion
    - ☐ b) a boar
    - ☐ c) a hawk
    - ☐ d) a bear

QUIZ 7
GENERAL KNOWLEDGE, MULTIPLE CHOICE

1. In the 1999 film *Galaxy Quest* which actor played Jason Nesmith, the actor who played Commander Peter Quincy Taggart?
   - ☐ a) Alan Rickman
   - ☐ b) Tim Allen
   - ☐ c) Tony Shalhoub
   - ☐ d) Jeremy Howard

2. In Frank Herbert's *Dune*, which kind of creatures are ridden by the native inhabitants of the titular planet?
   - ☐ a) Worms
   - ☐ b) Centipedes
   - ☐ c) Spiders
   - ☐ d) Scorpions

3. How many heads did Cerberus, the dog-like guardian of the Greek underworld, possess?
   - ☐ a) 1
   - ☐ b) 2
   - ☐ c) 3
   - ☐ d) 4

4. The character Black Canary features in comic books from which company?
   - ☐ a) Marvel
   - ☐ b) DC
   - ☐ c) Image
   - ☐ d) Dynamite

5. Which character in *The Lord of the Rings* is sometimes called "Elfstone"?
   - ☐ a) Gandalf
   - ☐ b) Aragorn
   - ☐ c) Legolas
   - ☐ d) Elrond

6. The evil "Umbrella Corporation" is found in which video game universe?

☐ a) *Half-Life*

☐ b) *BioShock*

☐ c) *Fallout*

☐ d) *Resident Evil*

7. Which *Buffy the Vampire Slayer* character is a werewolf?

☐ a) Rupert Giles

☐ b) Xander Harris

☐ c) Daniel "Oz" Osbourne

☐ d) Spike

8. The 2009 film *Avatar* is set on which moon?

☐ a) Pandora

☐ b) Eden

☐ c) Ariadne

☐ d) Endor

9. Who is the protagonist of the video game *The Legend of Zelda*?

☐ a) Stygg

☐ b) Droog

☐ c) Karn

☐ d) Link

10. Which of these *Red Dwarf* characters spent most of the series as a hologram?

☐ a) David Lister

☐ b) Arnold Rimmer

☐ c) Kristine Kochanski

☐ d) Kryten

QUIZ 8
GENERAL KNOWLEDGE, TRUE OR FALSE

1. All of the main characters of *Cowboy Bebop* are human/animal hybrids.
   ☐ True   ☐ False

2. Dragonlance is a setting for *Dungeons & Dragons*.
   ☐ True   ☐ False

3. The Thing was a founding member of the Fantastic Four.
   ☐ True   ☐ False

4. A griffin is a legendary animal that is half eagle and half bear.
   ☐ True   ☐ False

5. Tarzan's real name is John Clayton, Viscount Greystoke.
   ☐ True   ☐ False

6. Han Solo is the first human character to appear on screen in *The Empire Strikes Back*.
   ☐ True   ☐ False

7. Beast was one of the original X-Men.
   ☐ True   ☐ False

8. Sarah Michelle Gellar was originally cast in the role of Kate on *Lost* but had to drop out due to other commitments.
   ☐ True   ☐ False

9. Hermione Granger has one brother and one sister.
   ☐ True   ☐ False

10. Ursula K. Le Guin wrote *The Mists of Avalon*.
    ☐ True   ☐ False

QUIZ 9
GENERAL KNOWLEDGE QUESTIONS, SHORT ANSWER

1. What is the only science-fiction adventure television series to produce over 500 episodes?

    ....

2. What is the full title of the third film in the *Mad Max* series?

    ....

3. *The Colour of Magic* is the first book in what long-running fantasy series?

    ....

4. *Xena: Warrior Princess* was a spin-off from what television show?

    ....

5. Which show aired on television first, *The Twilight Zone* or *The Outer Limits*?

    ....

6. Complete this line from the opening of *Star Wars: A New Hope*: "A long time ago..."

    ....

7. What video game series includes human super-soldiers known as "Spartans"?

    ....

8. The character Judge Dredd from the comic book *2000 AD* operates in what city?

    ....

9. NGE is an acronym for what popular anime series?

    ....

10. From what London train station can you get the Hogwarts Express?

    ....

QUIZ 10
FANTASY AUTHORS AND THEIR CHARACTERS, MATCH UP

Match each of these characters from fantasy literature with the author who created them.

1. Jon Snow	a) Fritz Leiber
2. Solomon Kane	b) Robert E. Howard
3. Harry Potter	c) David Gemmell
4. Fafhrd and the Gray Mouser	d) C. S. Lewis
5. Lyra Belacqua	e) J. R. R. Tolkien
6. Druss the Legend	f) Stephen R. Donaldson
7. Aragorn	g) Philip Pullman
8. Roland Deschain	h) George R. R. Martin
9. Thomas Covenant	i) Stephen King
10. Aslan	j) J. K. Rowling

QUIZ 11
GENERAL KNOWLEDGE, MULTIPLE CHOICE

1. Which of these movie heroes was NOT portrayed by Kurt Russell?
   - ☐ a) Jack Burton
   - ☐ b) Snake Plissken
   - ☐ c) Col. Jack O'Neil
   - ☐ d) Rick Deckard

2. What is the third and final book in Philip Pullman's *His Dark Materials* trilogy?
   - ☐ a) *The Amber Spyglass*
   - ☐ b) *The Golden Compass*
   - ☐ c) *The Subtle Knife*
   - ☐ d) *Northern Lights*

3. In the television show *Fringe*, the Fringe is a Division of which organization?
   - ☐ a) FBI
   - ☐ b) CIA
   - ☐ c) DEA
   - ☐ d) Treasury Department

4. Who invented Conan the Barbarian?
   - ☐ a) L. Sprague de Camp
   - ☐ b) H. P. Lovecraft
   - ☐ c) Lin Carter
   - ☐ d) Robert E. Howard

5. Which of these was NOT one of the Teenage Mutant Ninja Turtles?
   - ☐ a) Donatello
   - ☐ b) Leonardo
   - ☐ c) Rembrandt
   - ☐ d) Raphael

6. Roland Deschain is the main character in which Stephen King novel?
   - ☐ a) *The Running Man*
   - ☐ b) *It*
   - ☐ c) *The Gunslinger*
   - ☐ d) *Dreamcatcher*

7. What is the first name of Kurt Russell's character in the film *Big Trouble in Little China*?
   - ☐ a) Dirk
   - ☐ b) Leroy
   - ☐ c) Jack
   - ☐ d) Michael

8. Who wrote the *Strange Case of Dr. Jekyll and Mr. Hyde*?
   - ☐ a) Edgar Alan Poe
   - ☐ b) Robert Louis Stevenson
   - ☐ c) Arthur Conan Doyle
   - ☐ d) Bram Stoker

9. Who played Van Helsing in the 2004 film of the same name?
   - ☐ a) Hugh Jackman
   - ☐ b) Tom Hardy
   - ☐ c) Russell Crowe
   - ☐ d) Daniel Craig

10. Who wrote *The Dying Earth* series?
   - ☐ a) John Jakes
   - ☐ b) L. Sprague de Camp
   - ☐ c) Jack Vance
   - ☐ d) Robert E. Howard

QUIZ 12
GENERAL KNOWLEDGE, MULTIPLE CHOICE

1. What is the nickname of the artificially intelligent computer in both the novel and film versions of *2001: A Space Odyssey*?
    - ☐ a) LEM
    - ☐ b) JIM
    - ☐ c) HAL
    - ☐ d) RON

2. According to Jim Butcher's *The Dresden Files*, Harry Dresden is the only wizard listed in the phone directory of which city?
    - ☐ a) New York
    - ☐ b) Chicago
    - ☐ c) Los Angeles
    - ☐ d) New Orleans

3. Which of these comic books has produced the most issues?
    - ☐ a) *The Amazing Spider-Man*
    - ☐ b) *Spider-Man*
    - ☐ c) *Peter Parker, The Spectacular Spider-Man*
    - ☐ d) *Sensational Spider-Man*

4. How many voyages did Sinbad the Sailor make?
    - ☐ a) 3
    - ☐ b) 5
    - ☐ c) 7
    - ☐ d) 9

5. Who wrote *A Connecticut Yankee in King Arthur's Court*?
    - ☐ a) Washington Irving
    - ☐ b) Mark Twain
    - ☐ c) Nathaniel Hawthorne
    - ☐ d) Ambrose Bierce

6. Who played the role of Dr. Peter Venkman in *Ghostbusters*?

☐ a) Bill Murray

☐ b) Dan Aykroyd

☐ c) Harold Ramis

☐ d) Rick Moranis

7. Who wrote *A Wrinkle in Time*?

☐ a) J. M. Barrie

☐ b) Richard Adams

☐ c) Cary Elwes

☐ d) Madeleine L'Engle

8. The 1954 film *Them!* features what type of giant bugs?

☐ a) spiders

☐ b) ants

☐ c) bees

☐ d) centipedes

9. What kind of animal is the protagonist in *Usagi Yojimbo*?

☐ a) a bear

☐ b) a monkey

☐ c) a rabbit

☐ d) a snake

10. Which DC Comics villain briefly served as President of the United States?

☐ a) T. O. Morrow

☐ b) Vandal Savage

☐ c) Black Adam

☐ d) Lex Luthor

QUIZ 13
GENERAL KNOWLEDGE, TRUE OR FALSE

1. According to *The Lord of the Rings*, Aragorn's father was Elendil.
   ☐ True   ☐ False

2. The original *Battlestar Galactica* series ran for only one season.
   ☐ True   ☐ False

3. *The Land that Time Forgot* was written by Arthur Conan Doyle.
   ☐ True   ☐ False

4. Author China Miéville is Canadian.
   ☐ True   ☐ False

5. *Star Wars: A New Hope* once held the record for highest grossing movie of all time.
   ☐ True   ☐ False

6. *How to Train Your Dragon* was a Pixar Animation Studios film.
   ☐ True   ☐ False

7. Percy Jackson is the son of Zeus.
   ☐ True   ☐ False

8. There are over 30 *Discworld* novels.
   ☐ True   ☐ False

9. Cthulhu is an "Elder God."
   ☐ True   ☐ False

10. The middle name of Buffy Summers, "the vampire slayer," is Julia.
    ☐ True   ☐ False

QUIZ 14
GENERAL KNOWLEDGE QUESTIONS, SHORT ANSWER

1. Who are the "heroes in a half-shell"?

   ....

2. In *Doctor Who*, what is the acronym TARDIS short for?

   ....

3. What legendary hero slew Grendel?

   ....

4. In *Back to the Future*, how much electric power is required to send the DeLorean through time?

   ....

5. In *Dungeons & Dragons*, what is the opposite alignment to Lawful Good?

   ....

6. On what spaceship would you be most likely to find David Lister, Arnold Rimmer, and The Cat?

   ....

7. What original series *Star Trek* character was played by DeForest Kelley?

   ....

8. In the *Terminator* film series, who is John Conner's father?

   ....

9. The character Drizzt Do'Urden is a member of what fantasy race?

   ....

10. Wilson Fisk is the real name of what Marvel Comics villain?

   ....

QUIZ 15
SUPERHEROES, MATCH UP

Match up these comic book superheroes with their alter egos.

1. The Batman

a) Al Simmons

2. Spider-Man

b) Wally West

3. Spawn

c) Arthur Curry

4. Green Lantern

d) Bruce Wayne

5. Captain America

e) Aric Dacia

6. X-O Manowar

f) Scott Summers

7. The Flash

g) Steve Rogers

8. Cyclops

h) Matt Murdock

9. Aquaman

i) Peter Parker

10. Daredevil

j) Hal Jordan

QUIZ 16
GENERAL KNOWLEDGE, MULTIPLE CHOICE

1. Queen Bavmorda was the principal villain in which fantasy film?
    - ☐ a) *Willow*
    - ☐ b) *Ladyhawke*
    - ☐ c) *The Little Mermaid*
    - ☐ d) *Labyrinth*

2. Which of these ambassadors to *Babylon 5* was a Narn?
    - ☐ a) Londo Mollari
    - ☐ b) G'Kar
    - ☐ c) Kosh
    - ☐ d) Delenn

3. Who was the first "Herald of Galactus" to appear in Marvel comics?
    - ☐ a) Silver Surfer
    - ☐ b) Firelord
    - ☐ c) Stardust
    - ☐ d) Red Shift

4. The King of Westeros sits upon which throne?
    - ☐ a) The Golden Throne
    - ☐ b) The Throne of Bronze
    - ☐ c) The Iron Throne
    - ☐ d) The Copper Throne

5. Which of these characters was not a companion of the Tenth Doctor as portrayed by David Tennant in *Doctor Who*?
    - ☐ a) Donna Noble
    - ☐ b) Martha Jones
    - ☐ c) Rose Tyler
    - ☐ d) Amelia Pond

6. In *Advanced Dungeons & Dragons* which level of spell is "Fireball"?
   - ☐ a) 1st
   - ☐ b) 3rd
   - ☐ c) 6th
   - ☐ d) 9th

7. Which of these actors did NOT star in the 1999 film *The Matrix*?
   - ☐ a) Hugo Weaving
   - ☐ b) Carrie-Anne Moss
   - ☐ c) Samuel L. Jackson
   - ☐ d) Joe Pantoliano

8. In *Stargate: SG-1*, when the team first meet Teal'c he is a servant of which Goa'uld?
   - ☐ a) Ba'al
   - ☐ b) Hathor
   - ☐ c) Anubis
   - ☐ d) Apophis

9. Who created the world of Xanth?
   - ☐ a) Robert Jordan
   - ☐ b) Terry Brooks
   - ☐ c) Piers Anthony
   - ☐ d) David Eddings

10. What is the first book in *The Dresden Files*?
    - ☐ a) *Storm Front*
    - ☐ b) *Death Masks*
    - ☐ c) *Full Moon*
    - ☐ d) *Grave Peril*

QUIZ 17
GENERAL KNOWLEDGE, MULTIPLE CHOICE

1. The American science-fiction icon "Robbie the Robot" first appeared in which film?
   - ☐ a) *The Black Hole*
   - ☐ b) *Plan 9 from Outer Space*
   - ☐ c) *Battle Beyond the Stars*
   - ☐ d) *Forbidden Planet*

2. Who is the main character of Neil Gaiman's *Sandman* comic series?
   - ☐ a) Sleep
   - ☐ b) Dream
   - ☐ c) Nightmare
   - ☐ d) Trance

3. In the television show *Firefly*, what nickname was given to the rebels who fought against the Alliance?
   - ☐ a) Browncoats
   - ☐ b) Redshirts
   - ☐ c) Bluecoats
   - ☐ d) Blueshirts

4. Which of these bounty hunters did not appear in *The Empire Strikes Back*?
   - ☐ a) Dengar
   - ☐ b) Boba Fett
   - ☐ c) Aurra Sing
   - ☐ d) Bossk

5. Which of these television series produced the most episodes?
   - ☐ a) *Star Trek*
   - ☐ b) *Star Trek: The Next Generation*
   - ☐ c) *Star Trek: Deep Space Nine*
   - ☐ d) *Star Trek: Voyager*

6. In the television show *Futurama*, how many eyes does the character Leela have?

☐ a) 1
☐ b) 2
☐ c) 3
☐ d) 4

7. What was the real name of the original Robin, the sidekick of Batman?

☐ a) Jason Todd
☐ b) Tim Drake
☐ c) Damian Wayne
☐ d) Dick Grayson

8. For how many seasons did *Buffy the Vampire Slayer* run?

☐ a) 5
☐ b) 6
☐ c) 7
☐ d) 8

9. How many books make up *Lemony Snicket's A Series of Unfortunate Events*?

☐ a) 13
☐ b) 15
☐ c) 17
☐ d) 19

10. Which of these is NOT an unforgivable curse?

☐ a) *Imperio*
☐ b) *Crucio*
☐ c) *Cunfundo*
☐ d) *Avada Kedavra*

QUIZ 18
GENERAL KNOWLEDGE, TRUE OR FALSE

1. There is no familial relationship between the Marvel Comics characters Hulk and She-Hulk.
   ☐ True ☐ False

2. The television show *Star Trek: Voyager* is mostly set outside of the Milky Way galaxy.
   ☐ True ☐ False

3. The film *Ghost in the Shell* is set in the year 2001.
   ☐ True ☐ False

4. In Greek myth, Medusa was one of the creatures known as "Gorgons."
   ☐ True ☐ False

5. The character Conan the Barbarian first appeared in the magazine *Weird Tales*.
   ☐ True ☐ False

6. J. R. R. Tolkien invented the word "orc."
   ☐ True ☐ False

7. Orion was a god of Ancient Greece.
   ☐ True ☐ False

8. Richard Garfield created the game *Munchkin*.
   ☐ True ☐ False

9. Quidditch teams are made up of seven players.
   ☐ True ☐ False

10. Michael J. Fox provided the voice for Milo James Thatch, the protagonist in Disney's *Atlantis: The Lost Empire*.
    ☐ True ☐ False

QUIZ 19
GENERAL KNOWLEDGE QUESTIONS, SHORT ANSWER

1. At what temperature, in Fahrenheit, does paper ignite?

    ....

2. What type of game is a LARP?

    ....

3. According to the writings of H. P. Lovecraft, where does dead Cthulhu wait dreaming?

    ....

4. What actor played the titular character in the 1976 film *Logan's Run*?

    ....

5. What British television program, which first aired in 1967, featured a protagonist known only as "Number Six"?

    ....

6. What television show title is sometimes abbreviated as "MST3K"?

    ....

7. In Greek mythology, what was the name of Daedalus' son who plunged to his death in the ocean after flying too close to the sun?

    ....

8. Is the television show *Lexx* named after a spaceship or a person?

    ....

9. *World's Finest Comics* mainly featured which two famous superheroes?

    ....

10. How many lions were needed to form the original Voltron?

    ....

QUIZ 20
HOME WORLDS, MATCH UP

Connect these science-fiction characters to their home worlds.

1. Spock

a) Furya

2. The Doctor

b) Gallifrey

3. Kosh

c) Chulak

4. Luke Skywalker

d) Corellia

5. Riddick

e) Earth

6. Inara Serra

f) Vulcan

7. Teal'c

g) Cybertron

8. Optimus Prime

h) Sihnon

9. Han Solo

i) Tatooine

10. James T. Kirk

j) Vorlon

QUIZ 21
GENERAL KNOWLEDGE, MULTIPLE CHOICE

1. In *Star Trek: Deep Space Nine*, which is the closest planet to the titular space station?
   - ☐ a) Vulcan
   - ☐ b) Klingon
   - ☐ c) Cardassia Prime
   - ☐ d) Bajor

2. Which of the following was NOT one of the ghosts in *Pac-Man*?
   - ☐ a) Pinky
   - ☐ b) Dinky
   - ☐ c) Inky
   - ☐ d) Clyde

3. What is the name of Boba Fett's spaceship in *The Empire Strikes Back*?
   - ☐ a) *Executioner*
   - ☐ b) *Prisoner II*
   - ☐ c) *The Cage*
   - ☐ d) *Slave I*

4. According to Marvel Comics, who is "The Man Without Fear"?
   - ☐ a) Batman
   - ☐ b) Wolverine
   - ☐ c) Daredevil
   - ☐ d) Captain America

5. The first episode of the original *Doom* video game was set on which planet?
   - ☐ a) Earth
   - ☐ b) Mars
   - ☐ c) Venus
   - ☐ d) Mercury

6. In the television series *Agents of S.H.I.E.L.D.*, which character is nicknamed "The Cavalry"?

☐ a) Grant Ward

☐ b) Melinda May

☐ c) Lance Hunter

☐ d) Jemma Simmons

7. Who wrote the 1969 novel *The Left Hand of Darkness*?

☐ a) Margaret Atwood

☐ b) Octavia Butler

☐ c) Ursula K. Le Guin

☐ d) Marge Piercy

8. Which character in *The Addams Family* was just a hand?

☐ a) It

☐ b) Thing

☐ c) Lurch

☐ d) Uncle Fester

9. Which of these characters from the original *Star Trek* series wasn't introduced until the second season?

☐ a) Pavel Chekov

☐ b) Hikaru Sulu

☐ c) Montgomery Scott

☐ d) Nyota Uhura

10. In which decade was the Disney animated feature *The Sword in the Stone* released?

☐ a) 1950s

☐ b) 1960s

☐ c) 1970s

☐ d) 1980s

QUIZ 22
GENERAL KNOWLEDGE, MULTIPLE CHOICE

1. In the 1994 film *Stargate*, in which country is the stargate discovered?
   - ☐ a) Egypt
   - ☐ b) Canada
   - ☐ c) Mexico
   - ☐ d) Japan

2. In Spider-Man comics, who is the editor-in-chief of the *Daily Bugle*?
   - ☐ a) Charles "Charley" Snow
   - ☐ b) Flash Thompson
   - ☐ c) J. Jonah Jameson, Jr.
   - ☐ d) Albert Jack Dickson

3. Who plays Rick Grimes in *The Walking Dead* television series?
   - ☐ a) Norman Reedus
   - ☐ b) Jeffery DuMunn
   - ☐ c) Jon Berthnal
   - ☐ d) Andrew Lincoln

4. Who invented the comic book character Spawn?
   - ☐ a) Marc Silvestri
   - ☐ b) Todd McFarlane
   - ☐ c) Jim Lee
   - ☐ d) Rob Liefeld

5. What color is the outfit worn by the Phantom, "The Ghost Who Walks"?
   - ☐ a) red
   - ☐ b) blue
   - ☐ c) purple
   - ☐ d) black

6. Who played Lt. Starbuck in the original 1978 series of *Battlestar Galactica*?

☐ a) Rick Springfield

☐ b) Lorne Green

☐ c) Dirk Benedict

☐ d) Richard Hatch

7. In *Star Trek: First Contact*, which alien race is the first to contact humans?

☐ a) Xindi

☐ b) Romulans

☐ c) Vulcans

☐ d) Klingons

8. Who wrote *The Hero and the Crown*?

☐ a) Stephenie Meyer

☐ b) Robin McKinley

☐ c) Trudi Canavan

☐ d) J. K. Rowling

9. In which science-fiction universe would you be most likely to find a "Jefferies Tube"?

☐ a) *Doctor Who*

☐ b) *Star Wars*

☐ c) *Stargate*

☐ d) *Star Trek*

10. Robert E. Howard was born and lived for most of his life in which state?

☐ a) Texas

☐ b) California

☐ c) Vermont

☐ d) Washington

QUIZ 23
GENERAL KNOWLEDGE, TRUE OR FALSE

1. L. Frank Baum wrote over a dozen books set in the world of Oz.
   ☐ True   ☐ False

2. The *Dragon* magazine, which supported the *Dungeons & Dragons* role-playing game, ran for over five hundred print issues.
   ☐ True   ☐ False

3. *Babylon 5* was the last of the Babylon stations.
   ☐ True   ☐ False

4. In *Buffy the Vampire Slayer*, Buffy's little sister Dawn does not appear until season 5.
   ☐ True   ☐ False

5. A pilot episode of the television show *Star Trek: Federation Marines* was filmed but never released.
   ☐ True   ☐ False

6. Glóin is the only living dwarf from *The Hobbit* to appear in *The Lord of the Rings*.
   ☐ True   ☐ False

7. Harry Potter has no middle name.
   ☐ True   ☐ False

8. The cast of the *Dungeons & Dragons* film that came out in 2000 includes Tom Baker playing an elf.
   ☐ True   ☐ False

9. The same author wrote *The Princess Bride* and *Lord of the Flies*.
   ☐ True   ☐ False

10. H. P. Lovecraft committed suicide.
   ☐ True   ☐ False

QUIZ 24
GENERAL KNOWLEDGE QUESTIONS, SHORT ANSWER

1. To whom does Mjölnir belong?

   ....

2. What actress played the title role in the *Wonder Woman* television series?

   ....

3. What do you need to be to capture a unicorn?

   ....

4. What is the name of the main character in Neal Stephenson's 1992 novel *Snow Crash*?

   ....

5. "I am Tetsuo" is a famous line in what anime movie?

   ....

6. Who created the character Hellboy?

   ....

7. Who played the titular character in the 1996 film *Barb Wire*?

   ....

8. What book was subtitled "An Oral History of the Zombie War"?

   ....

9. Who wrote *Have Spacesuit, Will Travel*?

   ....

10. What role-playing game company produced the games set in "The World of Darkness"?

   ....

QUIZ 25
VIDEO GAME CHARACTERS, MATCH UP

Match up these characters with the video game, or game series, in which they starred.

1. Mario

a) *Metroid*

2. Lara Croft

b) *Halo*

3. Link

c) *God of War*

4. Master Chief

d) *Tomb Raider*

5. Marcus Fenix

e) *Street Fighter*

6. Dirk the Daring

f) *Half-Life*

7. Gordon Freeman, Ph.D.

g) *Gears of War*

8. Sagat

h) *Donkey Kong*

9. Samus Aran

i) *Dragon's Lair*

10. Kratos

j) *The Legend of Zelda*

QUIZ 26
GENERAL KNOWLEDGE, MULTIPLE CHOICE

1. Which of these novels was NOT written by Michael Crichton?
   - ☐ a) *The Andromeda Strain*
   - ☐ b) *Red Storm Rising*
   - ☐ c) *Congo*
   - ☐ d) *Sphere*

2. In which fantastical city do Fafhrd and the Gray Mouser first meet?
   - ☐ a) Hogsmeade
   - ☐ b) King's Landing
   - ☐ c) Lankhmar
   - ☐ d) Dol Amroth

3. What is the subtitle of the film *Star Trek V*?
   - ☐ a) *The Search for Spock*
   - ☐ b) *The Final Frontier*
   - ☐ c) *The Voyage Home*
   - ☐ d) *The Undiscovered Country*

4. According to Isaac Asimov's *I, Robot*, how many laws of robotics are there?
   - ☐ a) 3
   - ☐ b) 4
   - ☐ c) 5
   - ☐ d) 6

5. In *Star Wars: A New Hope*, what was the intended destination of the *Millennium Falcon*'s crew when it was captured by the Death Star?
   - ☐ a) Corellia
   - ☐ b) Coruscant
   - ☐ c) Yavin 4
   - ☐ d) Alderaan

6. Which of these films is NOT based on a story written by Philip K. Dick?
   ☐ a) *Lawnmower Man*
   ☐ b) *Total Recall*
   ☐ c) *Minority Report*
   ☐ d) *A Scanner Darkly*

7. The owl is usually associated with which ancient Greek goddess?
   ☐ a) Hera
   ☐ b) Aphrodite
   ☐ c) Artemis
   ☐ d) Athena

8. In which comic book did Superman makes his first appearance?
   ☐ a) *Action Comics* 1
   ☐ b) *Action Comics* 37
   ☐ c) *World's Best Comics* 1
   ☐ d) *World's Finest Comics* 37

9. Who played the titular character in Tim Burton's film *Beetlejuice*?
   ☐ a) Robin Williams
   ☐ b) Jeffrey Jones
   ☐ c) Alec Baldwin
   ☐ d) Michael Keaton

10. In which year was the science-fiction film *Metropolis* first released?
    ☐ a) 1927
    ☐ b) 1935
    ☐ c) 1942
    ☐ d) 1950

QUIZ 27
GENERAL KNOWLEDGE, MULTIPLE CHOICE

1. Which of these classic science-fiction novels was NOT written by Robert A. Heinlein?
   - ☐ a) *The Moon is a Harsh Mistress*
   - ☐ b) *Starship Troopers*
   - ☐ c) *Stranger in a Strange Land*
   - ☐ d) *Childhood's End*

2. What is the English slang term for the aliens in the 2009 film *District 9*?
   - ☐ a) Crisps
   - ☐ b) Crabs
   - ☐ c) Prawns
   - ☐ d) Roaches

3. In the novel *Frankenstein* by Mary Shelley, what is the first name of the man who creates the monsters?
   - ☐ a) Victor
   - ☐ b) Hugo
   - ☐ c) Kenneth
   - ☐ d) Reginald

4. In which year was the first episode of *Doctor Who* broadcast on the BBC?
   - ☐ a) 1958
   - ☐ b) 1963
   - ☐ c) 1968
   - ☐ d) 1973

5. In the Silver Age comics, Green Lantern rings were powerless against which color?
   - ☐ a) green
   - ☐ b) blue
   - ☐ c) red
   - ☐ d) yellow

6. In the novel *Ender's Game*, what is "Ender" Wiggin's actual first name?
   - ☐ a) Andrew
   - ☐ b) Byron
   - ☐ c) Christopher
   - ☐ d) Daniel

7. Which of these men has never been The Flash?
   - ☐ a) Jay Garrick
   - ☐ b) Barry Allen
   - ☐ c) Guy Gardner
   - ☐ d) Wally West

8. The "Locust Horde" is a group of aliens in which science-fiction video game franchise?
   - ☐ a) *Mass Effect*
   - ☐ b) *Portal*
   - ☐ c) *Gears of War*
   - ☐ d) *Halo*

9. Which character from George R. R. Martin's *A Song of Ice and Fire* series is also known as "Stormborn", "Mother of Dragons" and "Breaker of Chains"?
   - ☐ a) Sansa Stark
   - ☐ b) Daenerys Targaryen
   - ☐ c) Lysa Arryn
   - ☐ d) Cersei Lannister

10. In *Dungeons & Dragons*, the "Mind Flayer" is another name for which type of creature?
    - ☐ a) Xorn
    - ☐ b) Githyanki
    - ☐ c) Displacer Beast
    - ☐ d) Illithid

QUIZ 28
GENERAL KNOWLEDGE, TRUE OR FALSE

1. At one point, the heroine known as the Scarlet Witch was married to the robot, Vision.
   ☐ True ☐ False

2. Leonard Nimoy owned the rights to the *Star Trek* character Spock.
   ☐ True ☐ False

3. In the 1989 film *The Punisher*, the titular role was played by Dolph Lundgren.
   ☐ True ☐ False

4. The New York Public Library has a copy of the *Necronomicon* that it purchased in 1874.
   ☐ True ☐ False

5. The original 1968 film *Night of the Living Dead* was filmed in black and white.
   ☐ True ☐ False

6. *Star Trek: The Next Generation* and *Star Trek: Deep Space Nine* both ran for seven seasons.
   ☐ True ☐ False

7. *The Wonderful Flight to the Mushroom Planet* is completely set on Earth.
   ☐ True ☐ False

8. Isaac Asimov was a professor of biochemistry.
   ☐ True ☐ False

9. *Dead Until Dark* is the first novel narrated by Sookie Stackhouse.
   ☐ True ☐ False

10. One of Terry Pratchett's *Discworld* novels is entitled *Thud!*
    ☐ True ☐ False

QUIZ 29
GENERAL KNOWLEDGE QUESTIONS, SHORT ANSWER

1. What type of weapon does Luke Skywalker fire from his X-wing to destroy the first Death Star?

    ....

2. The phrase "Klaatu barada nikto" originally comes from what film?

    ....

3. What does "THAC0" stand for?

    ....

4. The title of the television show *Torchwood* was chosen because it was an anagram of what?

    ....

5. "What has it got in its pocketses?"

    ....

6. Which comic character came first, Swamp Thing or Man-Thing?

    ....

7. "What is the air-speed velocity of an unladen swallow?"

    ....

8. What film includes the line "Roads? Where we're going, we don't need roads."?

    ....

9. What does the acronym NIMH stand for in the title *The Rats of NIMH*?

    ....

10. How many rings for the Dwarf-lords in their halls of stone?

    ....

STAR TREK SPECIES, MATCH UP

Connect these characters from the *Star Trek* franchise with their race.

1. Kira Nerys		a) Talaxian
2. T'Pol		b) Ocampa
3. Gowron		c) Changeling
4. Odo		d) Ferengi
5. Lwaxana Troi		e) Vulcan
6. Neelix		f) Human
7. Dukat		g) Cardassian
8. Quark		h) Bajoran
9. Kes		i) Betazoid
10. Tasha Yar		j) Klingon

QUIZ 31
GENERAL KNOWLEDGE, MULTIPLE CHOICE

1. In which year was Anne Rice's *Interview with the Vampire* first published?
    - ☐ a) 1976
    - ☐ b) 1982
    - ☐ c) 1988
    - ☐ d) 1992

2. According to Jim Butcher's *The Dresden Files*, where does Harry's pal Bob live?
    - ☐ a) In a rundown hotel
    - ☐ b) In a skull
    - ☐ c) In an empty beer bottle
    - ☐ d) In a seashell

3. For how many issues did DC Comics' *Hellblazer* run?
    - ☐ a) 100
    - ☐ b) 200
    - ☐ c) 300
    - ☐ d) 400

4. The video game *Baldur's Gate* takes place in which *Dungeons & Dragons* world?
    - ☐ a) Forgotten Realms
    - ☐ b) Greyhawk
    - ☐ c) Dragonlance
    - ☐ d) Ravenloft

5. According to the television show *Doctor Who*, what is the home planet of the Cybermen?
    - ☐ a) Skaro
    - ☐ b) Telos
    - ☐ c) Varros
    - ☐ d) Mondas

6. In which year was the animated film *Akira* released?

    ☐ a) 1978

    ☐ b) 1988

    ☐ c) 1998

    ☐ d) 2008

7. While playing the role of Geordi La Forge in *Star Trek: The Next Generation*, LeVar Burton was also hosting which children's television show?

    ☐ a) *The Magic Roundabout*

    ☐ b) *Captain Kangaroo*

    ☐ c) *Reading Rainbow*

    ☐ d) *Sesame Street*

8. Who played the role of Elric the Huntsman in the 2012 film *Snow White and the Huntsman*?

    ☐ a) Chris Evans

    ☐ b) Chris Hemsworth

    ☐ c) Chris Pratt

    ☐ d) James Marsden

9. In which year was the film *WarGames* released?

    ☐ a) 1979

    ☐ b) 1983

    ☐ c) 1988

    ☐ d) 1993

10. In which country was Bender Rodriguez built?

    ☐ a) Mexico

    ☐ b) Honduras

    ☐ c) Chile

    ☐ d) Portugal

QUIZ 32
GENERAL KNOWLEDGE, MULTIPLE CHOICE

1. Which of these characters was NOT an original member of the league in the comic book version of *The League of Extraordinary Gentlemen*?
   ☐ a) Allan Quatermain
   ☐ b) The Invisible Man
   ☐ c) Dorian Gray
   ☐ d) Dr. Jekyll

2. According to Terry Pratchett, Discworld is supported on the backs of how many elephants?
   ☐ a) 1
   ☐ b) 2
   ☐ c) 3
   ☐ d) 4

3. In J. R. R. Tolkien's *The Fellowship of the Ring*, what is the name of Tom Bombadil's wife?
   ☐ a) Roselily
   ☐ b) Goldberry
   ☐ c) Springlily
   ☐ d) Roseberry

4. What was the name of the character played by Eliza Dushku in the television series *Dollhouse*?
   ☐ a) Lima
   ☐ b) Sierra
   ☐ c) Fox
   ☐ d) Echo

5. In issue 181 of the *Daredevil* comic book, the assassin Elektra was killed by which supervillain?
   ☐ a) Boomerang
   ☐ b) Foolkiller

☐ c) Bullseye

☐ d) Typhoid Mary

6. According to *Dungeons & Dragons*, a "Drow" is a subspecies of which fantastical species?

☐ a) Elf

☐ b) Dwarf

☐ c) Gnome

☐ d) Orc

7. Which of these novels was NOT written by Jules Verne?

☐ a) *From the Earth to the Moon*

☐ b) *The Island of Doctor Moreau*

☐ c) *Twenty Thousand Leagues Under the Sea*

☐ d) *Journey to the Center of the Earth*

8. Who is Harry Potter's godfather?

☐ a) Sirius Black

☐ b) Remus Lupin

☐ c) Peter Pettigrew

☐ d) Albus Dumbledore

9. In which year is the video game *BioShock* set?

☐ a) 1930

☐ b) 1940

☐ c) 1950

☐ d) 1960

10. How many episodes were made of the original *The Prisoner* series?

☐ a) 17

☐ b) 32

☐ c) 43

☐ d) 68

QUIZ 33
GENERAL KNOWLEDGE, TRUE OR FALSE

1. The 1985 film *Legend* was directed by Ridley Scott.
   ☐ True   ☐ False

2. *Jurassic Park* held the title for highest grossing movie of all time before being overtaken by *Titanic*.
   ☐ True   ☐ False

3. *The Addams Family* began life as a series of single-panel cartoons, many of which appeared in *The New Yorker* magazine.
   ☐ True   ☐ False

4. The character of Captain Nemo first appeared in a play.
   ☐ True   ☐ False

5. Starfleet Headquarters is located in Tampa, Florida.
   ☐ True   ☐ False

6. The rights to the Godzilla franchise were owned by Michael Jackson for nearly two decades.
   ☐ True   ☐ False

7. According to *The Lord of the Rings*, both humans and hobbits live in the village of Bree.
   ☐ True   ☐ False

8. Isaac Asimov was born in Russia.
   ☐ True   ☐ False

9. In *Dungeons & Dragons*, metallic dragons are usually evil.
   ☐ True   ☐ False

10. In the movie *Spaceballs*, Spaceball is the name of a planet.
    ☐ True   ☐ False

QUIZ 34
GENERAL KNOWLEDGE QUESTIONS, SHORT ANSWER

1. In the 1987 film *The Princess Bride*, how does Inigo Montoya recognize the man who killed his father?

....

2. Who does Peter Parker marry in *The Amazing Spider-Man Annual* #21?

....

3. Who played the role of Guinan in *Star Trek: The Next Generation*?

....

4. What is the answer to the riddle of the Sphinx?

....

5. In the *Halo* video game universe, what does the abbreviation ODST stand for?

....

6. The mercenary unit Hammer's Slammers are famous for employing what type of military hardware?

....

7. Spike Spiegel is the protagonist of what science-fiction anime series?

....

8. What was the first English-language magazine devoted solely to science-fiction stories?

....

9. In what role-playing game are you most likely to lose sanity?

....

10. Kirk or Picard?

....

QUIZ 35
ACTRESSES, MATCH UP

Match these television characters to the actresses who portrayed them.

1. Willow Rosenberg

2. Susan Ivanova

3. Aeryn Sun

4. Sookie Stackhouse

5. Tasha Yar

6. Kara "Starbuck" Thrace

7. Rose Tyler

8. Samantha Carter

9. Nyssa of Traken

10. Cordelia Chase

a) Katee Sackhoff

b) Claudia Black

c) Billie Piper

d) Denise Crosby

e) Sarah Sutton

f) Anna Paquin

g) Charisma Carpenter

h) Alyson Hannigan

i) Amanda Tapping

j) Claudia Christian

DIFFICULTY LEVEL: MEDIUM

QUIZ 36
GENERAL KNOWLEDGE, MULTIPLE CHOICE

1. The word "Strigoi" is sometimes used to describe which type of creature?
   - ☐ a) Werewolf
   - ☐ b) Alien
   - ☐ c) Yeti
   - ☐ d) Vampire

2. What is the name of Rick Grimes's son in both the comic and television version of *The Walking Dead*?
   - ☐ a) Rick Jr.
   - ☐ b) Carl
   - ☐ c) Shane
   - ☐ d) Merle

3. What was the name of Scott Bakula's character in the television series *Quantum Leap*?
   - ☐ a) Sam Beckett
   - ☐ b) Dean Stockwell
   - ☐ c) Al Calavicci
   - ☐ d) Henry Heimlich

4. According to Douglas Adams' *Hitchhiker's Guide to the Galaxy*, who invented the Pan-Galactic Gargle Blaster?
   - ☐ a) Ford Prefect
   - ☐ b) Slartibartfast
   - ☐ c) Zaphod Beeblebrox
   - ☐ d) Deep Thought

5. In which television show were you most likely to encounter Sleestaks?
   - ☐ a) *Space 1999*
   - ☐ b) *Land of the Lost*
   - ☐ c) *Lexx*
   - ☐ d) *Star Trek: The Next Generation*

6. Which supervillain "killed" Superman in *Superman* (Vol. 2) #75 in 1992?

☐ a) Darkseid

☐ b) Doomsday

☐ c) Zod

☐ d) Lex Luthor

7. Which of Neil Gaiman's novels won the American Newbery Medal?

☐ a) *The Graveyard Book*

☐ b) *American Gods*

☐ c) *Good Omens*

☐ d) *Stardust*

8. In which year was *Buffy the Vampire Slayer* first broadcast?

☐ a) 1994

☐ b) 1997

☐ c) 2000

☐ d) 2002

9. What color is the outfit worn by the superhero known as "The Tick"?

☐ a) red

☐ b) blue

☐ c) green

☐ d) yellow

10. How old is Jon Snow when he first appears in the book *A Game of Thrones*?

☐ a) 14

☐ b) 18

☐ c) 20

☐ d) 24

QUIZ 37
GENERAL KNOWLEDGE, MULTIPLE CHOICE

1. In C. S. Lewis's *The Chronicles of Narnia*, which type of animal is Reepicheep?
   - ☐ a) a mouse
   - ☐ b) a dog
   - ☐ c) a cat
   - ☐ d) a deer

2. Which of these members of Red Squadron survives the attack on the Death Star in *Star Wars: A New Hope*?
   - ☐ a) Biggs Darklighter
   - ☐ b) Wedge Antilles
   - ☐ c) Jek Porkins
   - ☐ d) Garven Dreis

3. A hippogriff is a magical creature made up of a horse and which other animal?
   - ☐ a) a lion
   - ☐ b) a bear
   - ☐ c) an eagle
   - ☐ d) a serpent

4. In the 1982 film *E. T. the Extra-Terrestrial*, what is the name of Elliot's little sister?
   - ☐ a) Jannie
   - ☐ b) Mary
   - ☐ c) Lucy
   - ☐ d) Gertie

5. Who wrote the science-fiction and horror novel *The Night Land*?
   - ☐ a) Frank Belknap Long
   - ☐ b) H. P. Lovecraft
   - ☐ c) William Hope Hodgson
   - ☐ d) Clark Ashton Smith

6. Which of these characters from *Star Trek: Voyager* was NOT a member of the terrorist organization known as the Maquis?

☐ a) Chakotay

☐ b) B'Elanna Torres

☐ c) Harry Kim

☐ d) Tom Paris

7. In which year is *Neon Genesis Evangelion* set?

☐ a) 2015

☐ b) 2125

☐ c) 2345

☐ d) 2525

8. Which novel won both the Hugo Award and the Nebula Award in 2014?

☐ a) *Ancillary Justice* by Ann Leckie

☐ b) *Warbound* by Larry Correia

☐ c) *Parasite* by Mira Grant

☐ d) *Neptune's Brood* by Charles Stross

9. Who wrote "The Legend of Sleepy Hollow"?

☐ a) Nathaniel Hawthorn

☐ b) Washington Irving

☐ c) James Fenimore Cooper

☐ d) Edgar Alan Poe

10. In which science-fiction franchise is someone most likely to say "felgercarb"?

☐ a) *Babylon 5*

☐ b) *Battlestar Galactica*

☐ c) *Stargate*

☐ d) *Star Trek*

QUIZ 38
GENERAL KNOWLEDGE, TRUE OR FALSE

1. *Terminator: The Sarah Connor Chronicles* is set between the movies: *Terminator 2: Judgment Day* and *Terminator 3: Rise of the Machines*.
   ☐ True   ☐ False

2. The first episode of *Red Dwarf* is entitled "The End."
   ☐ True   ☐ False

3. The official name of the robot in *Lost in Space* was "CRIMP."
   ☐ True   ☐ False

4. In Marvel Comics, Captain Britain and Psylocke are brother and sister.
   ☐ True   ☐ False

5. Warwick Davis appears in Peter Jackson's film adaptation of *The Lord of the Rings*.
   ☐ True   ☐ False

6. The character of Boba Fett appeared on television before he appeared on film.
   ☐ True   ☐ False

7. In *Star Trek: The Next Generation* the USS *Enterprise* is a Constellation-class starship.
   ☐ True   ☐ False

8. Lewis Carroll never used the name "Mad Hatter" in any of the Alice stories.
   ☐ True   ☐ False

9. The phrase "All your base are belong to us" comes from the video game *Zero Wing*.
   ☐ True   ☐ False

10. Elvis Presley starred in a movie called *Teenage Robot*.
    ☐ True   ☐ False

QUIZ 39
GENERAL KNOWLEDGE QUESTIONS, SHORT ANSWER

1. In what year was the film *Dark Star* released?

    ....

2. What are the five basic colors of mana in *Magic: The Gathering*?

    ....

3. In *Return of the Jedi*, what creature inhabits the Great Pit of Carkoon?

    ....

4. What two men are credited with the creation of The Batman?

    ....

5. Who played the role of Dr. Leonard "Bones" McCoy in the 2009 film
    Star Trek?

    ....

6. Who played the monster in the 1931 film *Frankenstein*?

    ....

7. J'onn J'onzz is the real name of which DC Comics superhero?

    ....

8. In what world could you meet Tik-Tok, Rinkitink, and The Gump?

    ....

9. Who played Simon Phoenix in the 1993 film *Demolition Man*?

    ....

10. What does the acronym MMORPG stand for?

    ....

QUIZ 40
GAME OF THRONES, MATCH UP

Match these *Game of Thrones* characters with the actors who portray them.

1. Lord Eddard Stark

a) Iwan Rheon

2. Ramsay Snow

b) Aidan Gillen

3. Jon Snow

c) Lena Headey

4. Tormund Giantsbane

d) Natalie Dormer

5. Brienne of Tarth

e) Kristofer Hivju

6. Lord Petyr "Littlefinger" Baelish

f) Alfie Allen

7. Margaery Tyrell

g) Sean Bean

8. Daenerys Targaryen

h) Gwendoline Christie

9. Cersei Lannister

i) Emilia Clarke

10. Theon Greyjoy

j) Kit Harington

QUIZ 41
GENERAL KNOWLEDGE, MULTIPLE CHOICE

1. Which was the first book published in Robert Jordan's *The Wheel of Time* series?
   - ☐ a) *Crossroads of Twilight*
   - ☐ b) *The Path of Daggers*
   - ☐ c) *The Dragon Reborn*
   - ☐ d) *The Eye of the World*

2. How many *Star Trek* films featured the cast of *Star Trek: The Next Generation*?
   - ☐ a) 3
   - ☐ b) 4
   - ☐ c) 5
   - ☐ d) 6

3. According to Egyptian mythology, Horus is usually the son of which god?
   - ☐ a) Set
   - ☐ b) Ra
   - ☐ c) Osiris
   - ☐ d) Thoth

4. What was the name of the character played by Jessica Alba in the television series *Dark Angel*?
   - ☐ a) Elizabeth Renfro
   - ☐ b) Lucy Barrett
   - ☐ c) Hannah Sukova
   - ☐ d) Max Guevara

5. What is the last name of Batman's butler, Alfred?
   - ☐ a) Farthing
   - ☐ b) Alexander
   - ☐ c) Worthington
   - ☐ d) Pennyworth

6. Which actor plays the title character in the 1982 movie *Tron*?

- [ ] a) Jeff Bridges
- [ ] b) Bruce Boxleitner
- [ ] c) Peter Jurasik
- [ ] d) Bruce Campbell

7. Which Marvel character is sometimes called "The Merc with a Mouth"?

- [ ] a) Silver Sable
- [ ] b) Paladin
- [ ] c) Foolkiller
- [ ] d) Deadpool

8. In which city is the vampire hunter, Anita Blake, based?

- [ ] a) New Orleans
- [ ] b) St. Louis
- [ ] c) Baton Rogue
- [ ] d) Vicksburg

9. In which city is Torchwood Three based?

- [ ] a) Manchester
- [ ] b) Cardiff
- [ ] c) Edinburgh
- [ ] d) London

10. Which dimension did Buckaroo Bonzai adventure across?

- [ ] a) 4th
- [ ] b) 5th
- [ ] c) 6th
- [ ] d) 8th

QUIZ 42
GENERAL KNOWLEDGE, MULTIPLE CHOICE

1. For how many seasons did *Star Trek: Enterprise* run?
   - ☐ a) 3
   - ☐ b) 4
   - ☐ c) 5
   - ☐ d) 6

2. Galahad was the son of which Knight of the Round Table?
   - ☐ a) Gawain
   - ☐ b) Lancelot
   - ☐ c) Percival
   - ☐ d) Bors

3. The Marvel character, Black Widow, first appeared in which comic book?
   - ☐ a) *Iron Man*
   - ☐ b) *The Avengers*
   - ☐ c) *The Amazing Spider-Man*
   - ☐ d) *Tales of Suspense*

4. In the 1984 film, *The Terminator*, the titular cybernetic assassin travels back in time from which year?
   - ☐ a) 2012
   - ☐ b) 2029
   - ☐ c) 2089
   - ☐ d) 2101

5. The novel *Metro 2033* is predominately set in the subway of which city?
   - ☐ a) Moscow
   - ☐ b) New York
   - ☐ c) Paris
   - ☐ d) London

6. According to Jim Butcher's *The Dresden Files*, what is the "Blue Beetle"?

☐ a) Harry Dresden's favourite pub

☐ b) Harry Dresden's cat

☐ c) Harry Dresden's car

☐ d) Harry Dresden's staff

7. Which novel won the first ever Nebula Award for best science-fiction novel in 1966?

☐ a) *Dune* by Frank Herbert

☐ b) *All Flesh is Grass* by Clifford D. Simak

☐ c) *The Three Stigmata of Palmer Eldritch* by Philip K. Dick

☐ d) *A Plague of Demons* by Keith Laumer

8. "The Covenant" are an alliance of militaristic aliens in which video game franchise?

☐ a) *Gears of War*

☐ b) *Fallout*

☐ c) *Mass Effect*

☐ d) *Halo*

9. Who played King Arthur in the 1975 film *Monty Python and the Holy Grail*?

☐ a) John Cleese

☐ b) Graham Chapman

☐ c) Terry Jones

☐ d) Terry Gilliam

10. Azeroth is the world of which fantasy video game?

☐ a) *EverQuest*

☐ b) *World of Warcraft*

☐ c) *Myst*

☐ d) *Fable*

QUIZ 43
GENERAL KNOWLEDGE, TRUE OR FALSE

1. In *The Walking Dead* comics Rick Grimes loses his left hand.
   ☐ True   ☐ False

2. King Abdullah II of Jordan appeared in an episode of *Star Trek: Voyager*.
   ☐ True   ☐ False

3. Nick Fury first appeared in comic books during World War II.
   ☐ True   ☐ False

4. Warwick Davis had no acting experience before playing Wicket in *Return of the Jedi*.
   ☐ True   ☐ False

5. *The Hitchhiker's Guide to the Galaxy* was originally a radio drama before being turned into a novel.
   ☐ True   ☐ False

6. *Blade: The Series* ran for three seasons on three different channels in the USA.
   ☐ True   ☐ False

7. *Twenty Thousand Leagues Under the Sea* was the only novel written by Jules Verne to feature Captain Nemo.
   ☐ True   ☐ False

8. The television series *Blake's 7* was created by Terry Nation who also created the Daleks for *Doctor Who*.
   ☐ True   ☐ False

9. The 2012 Marvel film *The Avengers* was the highest grossing movie of all time.
   ☐ True   ☐ False

10. The actor Robert Picardo played a major character in both the *Star Trek* and *Stargate* universes.
    ☐ True   ☐ False

QUIZ 44
GENERAL KNOWLEDGE QUESTIONS, SHORT ANSWER

1. What non-human feature do female Gelflings have that male Gelflings do not?

   ....

2. Who created *Dungeons & Dragons* along with Gary Gygax?

   ....

3. What alien life-form, encountered in the original series of *Star Trek*, did Dr. Leonard McCoy conclude was "born pregnant"?

   ....

4. What is the more popular name of the "fifth dimension, beyond that which is known to man. It is a dimension as vast as space and as timeless as infinity. It is the middle ground between light and shadow, between science and superstition, and it lies between the pit of man's fears and the summit of his knowledge"?

   ....

5. How many films have been released starring the DC Comics character Swamp Thing?

   ....

6. Who created the *TekWar* series of novels?

   ....

7. What actor portrayed Deathstroke in the television show *Arrow* and Azog the Defiler in *The Hobbit* film series?

   ....

8. Is the film *Escape from L.A.* a prequel or a sequel to *Escape from New York*?

   ....

9. What science-fiction author wrote *Last and First Men*, *Odd John*, *Star Maker*, and *Sirius*?

....

10. What was the subtitle of the second *Highlander* film?

....

QUIZ 45
THE LORD OF THE RINGS ACTORS, MATCH UP

Match up these actors from Peter Jackson's *The Lord of the Rings* trilogy with the character they portrayed.

1. Billy Boyd   a) Grima

2. Bernard Hill   b) Celeborn

3. Andy Serkis   c) Theoden

4. David Wenham   d) Gamling

5. Brad Dourif   e) Haldir

6. John Noble   f) Denethor

7. Hugo Weaving   g) Elrond

8. Bruce Hopkins   h) Pippin

9. Craig Parker   i) Faramir

10. Marton Csokas   j) Gollum

QUIZ 46
GENERAL KNOWLEDGE, MULTIPLE CHOICE

1. In the *Watchmen* graphic novel, what is the real name of Dr. Manhattan?
   - ☐ a) Edward Morgan Blake
   - ☐ b) Jonathan Osterman
   - ☐ c) Daniel Dreiberg
   - ☐ d) Adrian Veidt

2. *Star Trek: The Next Generation* was set approximately how many years after the original *Star Trek* series?
   - ☐ a) 20
   - ☐ b) 50
   - ☐ c) 100
   - ☐ d) 250

3. In *Return of the Jedi*, which of these characters was NOT a performer in Jabba the Hutt's house band?
   - ☐ a) Max Rebo
   - ☐ b) Droopy McCool
   - ☐ c) Salacious B. Crumb
   - ☐ d) Sy Snootles

4. What is the name of the submarine in the 1960s television series *Voyage to the Bottom of the Sea*?
   - ☐ a) *Nautilus*
   - ☐ b) *Seaview*
   - ☐ c) *Skydiver*
   - ☐ d) *Cetacean*

5. Which Marvel superhero sometimes goes by the name "Joe Fixit"?
   - ☐ a) Hulk
   - ☐ b) Wolverine
   - ☐ c) The Punisher
   - ☐ d) Iron Fist

6. Drizzt Do'Urden is a character in which *Dungeons & Dragons* world?

☐ a) Ravenloft

☐ b) Eberron

☐ c) Greyhawk

☐ d) Forgotten Realms

7. What is the name of Leonard Nimoy's character in the television series *Fringe*?

☐ a) Dr. William Bell

☐ b) Brandon Fayette

☐ c) Captain Windmark

☐ d) Frank Stanton

8. Haymitch Abernathy is a character in which novel?

☐ a) *The Maze Runner*

☐ b) *Twilight*

☐ c) *The Hunger Games*

☐ d) *Mortal Engines*

9. In the television show *Smallville*, the town of Smallville is located in which state?

☐ a) Idaho

☐ b) Nebraska

☐ c) Iowa

☐ d) Kansas

10. Which of these is a name for a murderous fairy from British folklore?

☐ a) Redcap

☐ b) Bluecap

☐ c) Blackcap

☐ d) Whitecap

QUIZ 47
GENERAL KNOWLEDGE, MULTIPLE CHOICE

1. In David Lynch's 1984 movie adaptation of Frank Herbert's *Dune*, who portrayed Paul Atreides?
   - ☐ a) Jürgen Prochnow
   - ☐ b) Kyle MacLachlan
   - ☐ c) Patrick Stewart
   - ☐ d) Max von Sydow

2. In *Star Trek VI: The Undiscovered Country*, James T. Kirk is sentenced to life imprisonment on the mining asteroid Rura Penthe along with which other Enterprise officer?
   - ☐ a) Spock
   - ☐ b) Leonard McCoy
   - ☐ c) Hikaru Sulu
   - ☐ d) Montgomery Scott

3. According to the *Star Wars* franchise, which species is Jar Jar Binks?
   - ☐ a) Gungan
   - ☐ b) Dug
   - ☐ c) Neimoidian
   - ☐ d) Toydarian

4. Which television show, which first aired in 1959, was created and narrated by Rod Serling?
   - ☐ a) *The Outer Limits*
   - ☐ b) *Tales of Tomorrow*
   - ☐ c) *The Twilight Zone*
   - ☐ d) *Science Fiction Theatre*

5. Marvel Comics character Wolverine first appeared in a comic devoted to which other hero?
   - ☐ a) Captain America
   - ☐ b) Thor

☐ c) Spider-Man
☐ d) Hulk

6. In the television show *Heroes*, what power did police officer Matt Parkman possess?
   ☐ a) regeneration
   ☐ b) flight
   ☐ c) mind-reading
   ☐ d) mimicry

7. In *Buffy the Vampire Slayer*, which nightclub did Buffy visit regularly?
   ☐ a) the Gold
   ☐ b) the Silver
   ☐ c) the Bronze
   ☐ d) the Zinc

8. Who played Inigo Montoya in *The Princess Bride*?
   ☐ a) Cary Elwes
   ☐ b) Robin Wright
   ☐ c) Mandy Patinkin
   ☐ d) Anne Dyson

9. Which of the great houses of the Seven Kingdoms in *A Song of Ice and Fire* features a black stag on its coat of arms?
   ☐ a) House Baratheon
   ☐ b) House Greyjoy
   ☐ c) House Martell
   ☐ d) House Arryn

10. In which country would you be most likely to find the Fir Bolg?
    ☐ a) Canada
    ☐ b) Romania
    ☐ c) Greece
    ☐ d) Ireland

QUIZ 48
GENERAL KNOWLEDGE, TRUE OR FALSE

1. The DC Comics character Swamp Thing was created by Alan Moore.
   ☐ True   ☐ False

2. Peter Falk appears in the film *The Princess Bride*.
   ☐ True   ☐ False

3. The actor Michael Biehn, who appeared in films such as *The Terminator* and *Aliens,* has only one leg.
   ☐ True   ☐ False

4. Stan Lee claims to have based the looks and personality of comic book character Tony Stark on Howard Hughes.
   ☐ True   ☐ False

5. The magazine *Weird Tales* published its first issue in 1937.
   ☐ True   ☐ False

6. Peter Falk was once offered the lead role in *Doctor Who*.
   ☐ True   ☐ False

7. George R. R. Martin wrote more than a dozen episodes of the 1980s television show *Beauty and the Beast*.
   ☐ True   ☐ False

8. Fflewddur Fflam from *The Chronicles of Prydain* is a king.
   ☐ True   ☐ False

9. According to the 2007 film *Spider-Man 3*, Sandman killed Peter Parker's uncle Ben.
   ☐ True   ☐ False

10. The 1982 film *Tron* was released by Walt Disney Productions.
    ☐ True   ☐ False

QUIZ 49
GENERAL KNOWLEDGE QUESTIONS, SHORT ANSWER

1. What is the alternate title for Mary Shelley's 1818 novel *Frankenstein*?

   ....

2. Who directed the 1971 film, *THX 1138*?

   ....

3. In the book, *The Return of the King*, who led his Swan Knights in the defense of Minas Tirith?

   ....

4. The American cartoon *Star Blazers* was adapted from what Japanese anime?

   ....

5. According to *Babylon 5*, who was the only human to destroy a Minbari cruiser during the Earth-Minbari war?

   ....

6. The 1999 film *The 13th Warrior* is based on what book?

   ....

7. What comic book character's real name is Anung Un Rama?

   ....

8. In *The Empire Strikes Back*, what is the name of the rebel base on the planet Hoth?

   ....

9. Captain America's shield is made from what fictional metal?

   ....

10. What is a "jackalope"?

   ....

QUIZ 50
FANTASY AUTHORS AND THEIR CHARACTERS, MATCH UP

Match up these characters from fantasy literature with the author who created them.

1. Tarzan

a) H. P. Lovecraft

2. Victor Frankenstein

b) Terry Pratchett

3. Jack Pumpkinhead

c) Darren Shan

4. Captain Nemo

d) Jules Verne

5. Anita Blake

e) Charlaine Harris

6. Herbert West

f) Edgar Rice Burroughs

7. Rincewind

g) Stephenie Meyer

8. Sookie Stackhouse

h) Mary Shelley

9. Isabella Swan

i) Laurell K. Hamilton

10. Grubbs Grady

j) L. Frank Baum

QUIZ 51
GENERAL KNOWLEDGE, MULTIPLE CHOICE

1. In *Dungeons & Dragons* a "gnoll" appears to be the hybrid of a human and which animal?
    - ☐ a) a horse
    - ☐ b) a hyena
    - ☐ c) a hippopotamus
    - ☐ d) a heron

2. For how many seasons did *The X-Files* run?
    - ☐ a) 6
    - ☐ b) 7
    - ☐ c) 8
    - ☐ d) 9

3. What color was Mace Windu's lightsaber in the *Star Wars* franchise?
    - ☐ a) green
    - ☐ b) blue
    - ☐ c) red
    - ☐ d) violet

4. Which of the cast of *Mystery Science Theater 3000* has a head that closely resembles a gumball machine?
    - ☐ a) Crow T. Robot
    - ☐ b) Joel
    - ☐ c) Gypsy
    - ☐ d) Tom Servo

5. According to the legends, who was King Arthur's father?
    - ☐ a) Merlin
    - ☐ b) Vortigern
    - ☐ c) Uther Pendragon
    - ☐ d) King Lot

6. Which actress played the role of Sarah Connor in *Terminator: The Sarah Connor Chronicles*?
   - ☐ a) Summer Glau
   - ☐ b) Riley Dawson
   - ☐ c) Catherine Weaver
   - ☐ d) Lena Headey

7. Who is Superman's biological father?
   - ☐ a) Kal-El
   - ☐ b) Jor-El
   - ☐ c) Hatu-El
   - ☐ d) Gam-El

8. According to *Stargate: SG-1*, where is Stargate Command located?
   - ☐ a) Colorado Springs
   - ☐ b) San Antonio
   - ☐ c) White Sands
   - ☐ d) Area 51

9. Which of these books was NOT written by Joe Abercrombie?
   - ☐ a) *The Blade Itself*
   - ☐ b) *Inheritance*
   - ☐ c) *Best Served Cold*
   - ☐ d) *Red Country*

10. In the television show *Warehouse 13*, in which state is Warehouse 13 located?
   - ☐ a) Washington
   - ☐ b) Alaska
   - ☐ c) South Dakota
   - ☐ d) Wyoming

QUIZ 52
GENERAL KNOWLEDGE, MULTIPLE CHOICE

1. Which of these magical swords was wielded by Elric of Melniboné?
   - ☐ a) Stormbringer
   - ☐ b) Glamdring
   - ☐ c) The Sword of Truth
   - ☐ d) The Darksword

2. What was the name of Tommy Lee Jones's character in the 1997 film *Men in Black*?
   - ☐ a) Agent A
   - ☐ b) Agent Q
   - ☐ c) Agent K
   - ☐ d) Agent D

3. Which of these characters is NOT a core member of the DC superteam Birds of Prey?
   - ☐ a) Oracle
   - ☐ b) Huntress
   - ☐ c) Black Canary
   - ☐ d) Zatanna

4. In George Orwell's novel *1984*, what is the name of the island formerly known as Great Britain?
   - ☐ a) Oldspeak
   - ☐ b) Airstrip One
   - ☐ c) The Ministry
   - ☐ d) Jura

5. Which actor played the Doctor in the most episodes of *Doctor Who*?
   - ☐ a) William Hartnell
   - ☐ b) Tom Baker
   - ☐ c) Peter Davidson
   - ☐ d) Colin Baker

6. Who created the comic book character The Crow?
   - ☐ a) Herb Trimpe
   - ☐ b) David B. Schwartz
   - ☐ c) Denise O'Neil
   - ☐ d) James O'Barr

7. In *The Chronicles of Narnia*, which of these characters is a cousin to Lucy Pevensie?
   - ☐ a) Jill Pole
   - ☐ b) Eustace Scrubb
   - ☐ c) Digory Kirke
   - ☐ d) Polly Plummer

8. Which comic book character makes the noise "Bamf"?
   - ☐ a) Dazzler
   - ☐ b) Jubilee
   - ☐ c) Nightcrawler
   - ☐ d) Nova

9. In the television show *Futurama*, what is Fry's first name?
   - ☐ a) Philip
   - ☐ b) Jacob
   - ☐ c) Steven
   - ☐ d) Matt

10. Author Glen Cook wrote a series of novels chronicling the adventures of which elite mercenary unit?
   - ☐ a) Kell Hounds
   - ☐ b) Crazy Eights
   - ☐ c) The Black Company
   - ☐ d) Hammer's Slammers

QUIZ 53
GENERAL KNOWLEDGE, TRUE OR FALSE

1. The novel *She* was not published until after the death of the author, H. Rider Haggard.
   ☐ True   ☐ False

2. The comic book character Painkiller Jane had her own television series.
   ☐ True   ☐ False

3. Lord Dunsany was actually a baron.
   ☐ True   ☐ False

4. The main character of the manga and anime *Berserk* is named Guts.
   ☐ True   ☐ False

5. The 1995 film *12 Monkeys* is based on a book of the same name.
   ☐ True   ☐ False

6. Warwick Davis played multiple roles in the *Harry Potter* series of films.
   ☐ True   ☐ False

7. *The Fellowship of the Ring* was the first fantasy novel to appear on the *New York Times'* bestseller list.
   ☐ True   ☐ False

8. According to *Dungeons & Dragons*, a "Drider" is a creature that is half human and half snake.
   ☐ True   ☐ False

9. The actor David Wenham appears in the movies *The Lord of the Rings: The Return of the King*, *Van Helsing*, and *300*.
   ☐ True   ☐ False

10. "Egon Spengler" is the correct spelling of the name of the *Ghostbusters* character.
    ☐ True   ☐ False

QUIZ 54
GENERAL KNOWLEDGE QUESTIONS, SHORT ANSWER

MEDIUM

1. The planet Klendathu features in what science-fiction novel and film that share the same name?

   ....

2. What comic book company publishes *The Walking Dead*?

   ....

3. In the 1987 film *The Princess Bride*, what does R.O.U.S. stand for?

   ....

4. Which show had more total episodes, *Xena: Warrior Princess* or *Hercules: The Legendary Journeys*?

   ....

5. What regular cast member of *Lost in Space* also landed a regular role in *Babylon 5*?

   ....

6. According to the oath of the Green Lantern Corps, what is the next line after "In brightest day, in blackest night..."?

   ....

7. Who created the masked crime-fighter called "The Spirit"?

   ....

8. According to J. R. R. Tolkien, how many Silmarils were there?

   ....

9. Who created *Magic: The Gathering*?

   ....

10. What was the first English-language magazine dedicated to the publication of fantasy stories?

   ....

QUIZ 55
THORIN'S COMPANY, MATCH UP

Match up these dwarves from *The Hobbit* series of films with the actors who portrayed them.

1. Thorin Oakenshield   a) Mark Hadlow

2. Bofur   b) Ken Stott

3. Dori   c) Aidan Turner

4. Glóin   d) Graham McTavish

5. Bombur   e) Dean O'Gorman

6. Balin   f) Richard Armitage

7. Kíli   g) Peter Hambleton

8. Dwalin   h) James Nesbitt

9. Fíli   i) William Kircher

10. Bifur   j) Stephen Hunter

QUIZ 56
GENERAL KNOWLEDGE, MULTIPLE CHOICE

1. Who played the role of Roy Batty in the 1982 film *Blade Runner*?
   - ☐ a) Harrison Ford
   - ☐ b) Rutger Hauer
   - ☐ c) Brion James
   - ☐ d) Steven Seagal

2. What was the title of the *second* sequel to Douglas Adams' novel *The Hitchhiker's Guide to the Galaxy*?
   - ☐ a) *So Long, and Thanks for All the Fish*
   - ☐ b) *Mostly Harmless*
   - ☐ c) *Life, the Universe and Everything*
   - ☐ d) *The Restaurant at the End of the Universe*

3. Who played the character of Olivia Dunham in the television series *Fringe*?
   - ☐ a) Lily Pilblad
   - ☐ b) Blair Brown
   - ☐ c) Jasika Nicole
   - ☐ d) Anna Torv

4. Which of these ancient Greek gods was NOT a brother to the others?
   - ☐ a) Ares
   - ☐ b) Poseidon
   - ☐ c) Hades
   - ☐ d) Zeus

5. In which decade did Spider-Man first appear in comic books?
   - ☐ a) 1940s
   - ☐ b) 1950s
   - ☐ c) 1960s
   - ☐ d) 1970s

6. How many players could simultaneously play the arcade version of the video game *Gauntlet*?
   - ☐ a) 2
   - ☐ b) 3
   - ☐ c) 4
   - ☐ d) 5

7. Which of the "Robotech Wars" is also known as *The Macross Saga*?
   - ☐ a) First
   - ☐ b) Second
   - ☐ c) Third
   - ☐ d) Fourth

8. The Knight Sabers are an all-female mercenary outfit in which anime?
   - ☐ a) *Ghost in the Shell*
   - ☐ b) *Mobile Suit Gundam*
   - ☐ c) *Tank Police*
   - ☐ d) *Bubblegum Crisis*

9. The DC Comics heroine Oracle has what disability?
   - ☐ a) epilepsy
   - ☐ b) paraplegia
   - ☐ c) deafness
   - ☐ d) blindness

10. Which of these video games is NOT part of *The Elder Scrolls* series?
   - ☐ a) *Oblivion*
   - ☐ b) *Skyrim*
   - ☐ c) *Morrowind*
   - ☐ d) *Diablo*

QUIZ 57
GENERAL KNOWLEDGE, MULTIPLE CHOICE

1. Who directed the 1986 film *Star Trek IV: The Voyage Home*?
   - ☐ a) William Shatner
   - ☐ b) Leonard Nimoy
   - ☐ c) Nicholas Meyer
   - ☐ d) Robert Wise

2. According to the television show *Buck Rogers*, first broadcast in 1979, the titular hero traveled from the present day to which century?
   - ☐ a) 21st
   - ☐ b) 25th
   - ☐ c) 29th
   - ☐ d) 33rd

3. Which Greek hero kidnapped Helen of Sparta (later Helen of Troy) when she was a young girl?
   - ☐ a) Hercules
   - ☐ b) Jason
   - ☐ c) Perseus
   - ☐ d) Theseus

4. Which 1981 film has been described as "*High Noon* in space with Sean Connery"?
   - ☐ a) *The Quick and the Dead*
   - ☐ b) *Hellraiser*
   - ☐ c) *The Last Starfighter*
   - ☐ d) *Outland*

5. In the final issue of the original series of *Wonder Woman* comics, who did Wonder Woman marry?
   - ☐ a) Howard Shelton
   - ☐ b) Lyle Waggoner
   - ☐ c) Steve Trevor
   - ☐ d) George Newbern

6. What was Stephen King's first novel to see publication?
   - ☐ a) *'Salem's Lot*
   - ☐ b) *The Shining*
   - ☐ c) *Carrie*
   - ☐ d) *Rage*

7. In *The Empire Strikes Back*, above which planet is Cloud City located?
   - ☐ a) Bespin
   - ☐ b) Ord Mantell
   - ☐ c) Genosis
   - ☐ d) Dagobah

8. Ororo Munroe is the real name of which Marvel superhero?
   - ☐ a) Psylocke
   - ☐ b) X-23
   - ☐ c) Storm
   - ☐ d) Captain Marvel

9. In which real-world city would you find Lauren Beukes' *Zoo City*?
   - ☐ a) New York
   - ☐ b) Johannesburg
   - ☐ c) Tripoli
   - ☐ d) Manila

10. In which year was the original *Fallout* video game released?
   - ☐ a) 1997
   - ☐ b) 2000
   - ☐ c) 2003
   - ☐ d) 2006

QUIZ 58
GENERAL KNOWLEDGE, TRUE OR FALSE

1. *Star Trek: The Animated Series* ran for more than one season.
   ☐ True   ☐ False

2. The mini-series *V* was inspired by the Sinclair Lewis novel *It Can't Happen Here.*
   ☐ True   ☐ False

3. In 2013, Stephen King released a sequel to *The Shining* entitled *Mr. X.*
   ☐ True   ☐ False

4. In the television show *Cleopatra 2525*, the main character is put into suspended animation for 525 years after complications during her breast augmentation surgery.
   ☐ True   ☐ False

5. Kenny Baker played the role of R2-D2 in all of the first six *Star Wars* movies.
   ☐ True   ☐ False

6. Worldwide, Harry Potter books have sold over one billion copies.
   ☐ True   ☐ False

7. The 1974 film *Zardoz* was written, produced, and directed by John Boorman.
   ☐ True   ☐ False

8. George R. R. Martin wrote over half-a-dozen episodes of *Buffy the Vampire Slayer.*
   ☐ True   ☐ False

9. Both Arthur Conan Doyle and H. P. Lovecraft were friends with Harry Houdini.
   ☐ True   ☐ False

10. *The Magazine of Fantasy & Science Fiction* once published a short story written entirely by a chimpanzee.
    ☐ True   ☐ False

QUIZ 59
GENERAL KNOWLEDGE QUESTIONS, SHORT ANSWER

1. How many different varieties of dice came in the original *Dungeons & Dragons* box set?

    ....

2. What is the only novel by Walter M. Miller, Jr. published during his lifetime?

    ....

3. Who played Éomer in the Peter Jackson-directed film adaptations of *The Two Towers* and *The Return of the King*?

    ....

4. What was the name of the short-lived, 2010 television series that served as a prequel to *Battlestar Galactica*?

    ....

5. Yorick Brown is the protagonist of what comic book series?

    ....

6. In the Marvel Universe, Doctor Doom is the ruler of what country?

    ....

7. Fangorn is an alternate name for what character from *The Lord of the Rings*?

    ....

8. Who was Marvel Comics' original "Hero for Hire"?

    ....

9. What is the projected title of the seventh book in the *A Song of Ice and Fire* series?

    ....

10. What is the name for the symbol of a dragon or serpent eating its own tail?

    ....

QUIZ 60
NEBULA AWARD-WINNING NOVELS, MATCH UP

Match up these Nebula Award-winning novels with their authors.

1. *A Time of Changes*

a) Vonda M. McIntyre

2. *The Gods Themselves*

b) Robert Silverberg

3. *Man Plus*

c) Gregory Benford

4. *Timescape*

d) Pat Murphy

5. *Dreamsnake*

e) Samuel R. Delany

6. *The Einstein Intersection*

f) Isaac Asimov

7. *No Enemy But Time*

g) Alexei Panshin

8. *Falling Free*

h) Michael Bishop

9. *Rite of Passage*

i) Frederik Pohl

10. *The Falling Woman*

j) Lois McMaster Bujold

QUIZ 61
GENERAL KNOWLEDGE, MULTIPLE CHOICE

1. How old is Bruce Wayne when he comes out of retirement in *Batman: The Dark Knight Returns*?
   - ☐ a) 50
   - ☐ b) 55
   - ☐ c) 60
   - ☐ d) 65

2. What is the nickname of the 58th Squadron of United States Marine Corps Space Aviator Cavalry in the television show *Space: Above and Beyond*?
   - ☐ a) Snakes
   - ☐ b) Wild Weasels
   - ☐ c) Wildcards
   - ☐ d) Night Hunters

3. In the comic book *Savage Dragon*, the titular character is a member of the police force of which city?
   - ☐ a) Los Angeles
   - ☐ b) New York
   - ☐ c) Chicago
   - ☐ d) St. Louis

4. In the television show *Futurama*, which planet does Doctor Zoidberg come from?
   - ☐ a) Decapod 10
   - ☐ b) Colgate 8
   - ☐ c) Amphibios 9
   - ☐ d) Doohan 6

5. In which year was the first *Resident Evil* video game released?
   - ☐ a) 1996
   - ☐ b) 1999
   - ☐ c) 2001
   - ☐ d) 2004

6. In the television series *Arrow*, the character of Slade Wilson is based on which DC Comics character?
   - ☐ a) The Flash
   - ☐ b) Cyborg
   - ☐ c) Deathstroke
   - ☐ d) Blue Beetle

7. The Marvel mutant, Jean Grey, originally appeared in the *X-Men* using which superhero name?
   - ☐ a) Marvel Girl
   - ☐ b) Marvel Woman
   - ☐ c) Power Woman
   - ☐ d) Wonder Woman

8. What was the real name of Sylar, the character portrayed by Zachary Quinto in *Heroes*?
   - ☐ a) Gordon Gray
   - ☐ b) Guy Gray
   - ☐ c) Gerald Grey
   - ☐ d) Gabriel Gray

9. The occultist John Dee was an advisor to which monarch?
   - ☐ a) James I
   - ☐ b) Charles I
   - ☐ c) Elizabeth I
   - ☐ d) Henry VIII

10. Which of the *A Song of Ice and Fire* novels had the longest page count in the original US editions?
   - ☐ a) *A Storm of Swords*
   - ☐ b) *A Feast for Crows*
   - ☐ c) *A Clash of Kings*
   - ☐ d) *A Dance with Dragons*

QUIZ 62
GENERAL KNOWLEDGE, MULTIPLE CHOICE

1. According to the television show *Firefly*, who is the "Hero of Canton"?
   - ☐ a) Malcolm Reynolds
   - ☐ b) Zoe Washburne
   - ☐ c) Derrial Book
   - ☐ d) Jayne Cobb

2. What is the alternate title for Kurt Vonnegut's novel *Slaughterhouse Five*?
   - ☐ a) *A Travel Through Time*
   - ☐ b) *The Firestorm*
   - ☐ c) *The Children's Crusade: A Duty-Dance with Death*
   - ☐ d) *Contract Labor*

3. In *Star Trek: Deep Space Nine*, what is the name of Quark's brother?
   - ☐ a) Rom
   - ☐ b) Nog
   - ☐ c) Zek
   - ☐ d) Gross

4. Oswald Chesterfield Cobblepot is the real name of which Batman villain?
   - ☐ a) Two-Face
   - ☐ b) Joker
   - ☐ c) Penguin
   - ☐ d) Ra's al Ghul

5. The Marvel character The Punisher first appeared in which comic book?
   - ☐ a) *Captain America*
   - ☐ b) *The Amazing Spider-Man*
   - ☐ c) *Iron Man*
   - ☐ d) *Daredevil*

6. In which series of *Red Dwarf* does Kryten first appear?
    ☐ a) I
    ☐ b) II
    ☐ c) III
    ☐ d) IV

7. What is Judge Dredd's first name?
    ☐ a) Jonah
    ☐ b) Jeremiah
    ☐ c) Joseph
    ☐ d) John

8. Which of these science-fiction films was NOT directed by Paul Verhoeven?
    ☐ a) *RoboCop*
    ☐ b) *The Running Man*
    ☐ c) *Starship Troopers*
    ☐ d) *Total Recall*

9. Which of these characters in *Buffy the Vampire Slayer* was also a "Slayer"?
    ☐ a) Tara Maclay
    ☐ b) Jenny Calendar
    ☐ c) Joyce Summers
    ☐ d) Kendra Young

10. Which of these films was NOT directed by Terry Gilliam?
    ☐ a) *Time Bandits*
    ☐ b) *12 Monkeys*
    ☐ c) *Brazil*
    ☐ d) *Logan's Run*

QUIZ 63
GENERAL KNOWLEDGE, TRUE OR FALSE

1. The novel *Ender's Game* and its sequel, *Speaker for the Dead*, both won the Hugo and the Nebula Awards in back-to-back years.
   ☐ True   ☐ False

2. The movie *Logan's Run* spawned a short-lived television series.
   ☐ True   ☐ False

3. All three seasons of *Lost in Space* were filmed in black and white and later colorized.
   ☐ True   ☐ False

4. Jim Gordon of the Gotham City Police Department made his first appearance in *Detective Comics* #27, more famous for the first appearance of Batman.
   ☐ True   ☐ False

5. In the 1980s, the American actor Gene Wilder was offered the role of the Doctor in *Doctor Who* but turned it down.
   ☐ True   ☐ False

6. Sigourney Weaver is among the voice actors who contributed to the 2008 animated film *WALL-E*.
   ☐ True   ☐ False

7. The DC Comics character Green Arrow first appeared in issue 73 of *More Fun Comics*.
   ☐ True   ☐ False

8. In *The Lord of the Rings*, Aragorn is older than Bilbo Baggins.
   ☐ True   ☐ False

9. Sean Pertwee played Robert Muldoon, the park's game warden, in the film *Jurassic Park*.
   ☐ True   ☐ False

10. None of the *A Song of Ice and Fire* novels have won the Nebula Award.
    ☐ True   ☐ False

QUIZ 64
GENERAL KNOWLEDGE QUESTIONS, SHORT ANSWER

1. What weapon is used to slay the Jabberwocky in the poem by Lewis Carroll?

....

2. In the *A Song of Ice and Fire* series, what character's name is an anagram of "a merry dance"?

....

3. What is the first book of Christopher Paolini's *Inheritance Cycle*?

....

4. What monstrous creature will kill the Norse god Thor during Ragnarök?

....

5. What is the name of the character played by Claudia Black in *Stargate: SG-1*?

....

6. The Machinima comedy series *Red vs. Blue* is based on what video game?

....

7. According to the Marvel Comics mini-series *Origin*, what was Wolverine's birth name?

....

8. What movie features the characters Korben Dallas, Leeloo, and Jean-Baptiste Emanuel Zorg?

....

9. Hyrule is the fantasy world setting for what video game series?

....

10. Who provided the voice for Tony Stark's computerized A.I. J.A.R.V.I.S. in the *Iron Man* films?

....

QUIZ 65
FANTASY WORLDS, MATCH UP

Match up these fantasy worlds with the authors who created them.

1. Pern	a) Terry Pratchett
2. Nehwon	b) Roger Zelazny
3. Shannara	c) Anne McCaffrey
4. Discworld	d) Raymond E. Feist
5. Barsoom	e) Guy Gavriel Kay
6. Amber	f) Edgar Rice Burroughs
7. Xanth	g) C. S. Lewis
8. Midkemia	h) Fritz Leiber
9. Narnia	i) Piers Anthony
10. Fionavar	j) Terry Brooks

DIFFICULTY LEVEL: HARD

QUIZ 66
GENERAL KNOWLEDGE, MULTIPLE CHOICE

1. Who wrote *The Liveship Traders Trilogy*?
   - ☐ a) Robert Holdstock
   - ☐ b) Jonathan Stroud
   - ☐ c) Brandon Sanderson
   - ☐ d) Robin Hobb

2. In which year was J. R. R. Tolkien's *The Silmarillion* first published?
   - ☐ a) 1960
   - ☐ b) 1969
   - ☐ c) 1977
   - ☐ d) 1984

3. A "skaven" is a mutated version of which animal?
   - ☐ a) a dog
   - ☐ b) a rat
   - ☐ c) a lizard
   - ☐ d) a wolf

4. Which *Doctor Who* companion died at the end of the 1982 serial *Earthshock*?
   - ☐ a) Tegan
   - ☐ b) Nyssa
   - ☐ c) Turlough
   - ☐ d) Adric

5. What is the third and final book in Kim Stanley Robinson's *Martian Trilogy*?
   - ☐ a) *Red Mars*
   - ☐ b) *Green Mars*
   - ☐ c) *Blue Mars*
   - ☐ d) *Yellow Mars*

6. In which year was the video game *EverQuest* first released?
   - ☐ a) 1989
   - ☐ b) 1995
   - ☐ c) 1999
   - ☐ d) 2003

7. Tom Mason, the main character of the television series, *Falling Skies*, was a professor at which university before the alien invasion?
   - ☐ a) M.I.T.
   - ☐ b) Boston University
   - ☐ c) Yale
   - ☐ d) University of Maryland

8. Which of these Robert E. Howard characters appeared in print first?
   - ☐ a) Conan
   - ☐ b) Kull
   - ☐ c) Bran Mak Morn
   - ☐ d) Solomon Kane

9. What is the first book in *The Hungry City Chronicles* (also known as the *Predator Cities* series)?
   - ☐ a) *A Darkling Plain*
   - ☐ b) *Infernal Devices*
   - ☐ c) *Predator's Gold*
   - ☐ d) *Mortal Engines*

10. Which character did Barry Humphries portray in *The Hobbit: An Unexpected Journey*?
   - ☐ a) Bill the Troll
   - ☐ b) Yazneg
   - ☐ c) The Great Goblin
   - ☐ d) The Necromancer

QUIZ 67
GENERAL KNOWLEDGE, MULTIPLE CHOICE

1. Which role-playing games company originally published *Cyberpunk 2020*?
   - ☐ a) TSR
   - ☐ b) Steve Jackson Games
   - ☐ c) R. Talsorian Games
   - ☐ d) Palladium

2. What is the name of the mysterious creature who impales people on a giant metal tree in Dan Simmons' novel *Hyperion*?
   - ☐ a) The Crow
   - ☐ b) The Vulture
   - ☐ c) The Fiscal
   - ☐ d) The Shrike

3. According to *Star Trek: The Next Generation*, which ship was Jean-Luc Picard's first command?
   - ☐ a) USS *Stargazer*
   - ☐ b) USS *Constellation*
   - ☐ c) USS *Exeter*
   - ☐ d) USS *Lexington*

4. In the 1990s, which former Green Lantern became the supervillain Parallax?
   - ☐ a) Guy Gardner
   - ☐ b) Hal Jordan
   - ☐ c) Kyle Rayner
   - ☐ d) Alan Scott

5. According to the novel *A Fire Upon the Deep* by Vernor Venge, the planet Earth is in which "Zone of Thought"?
   - ☐ a) Unthinking Depths
   - ☐ b) Slow Zone
   - ☐ c) Beyond
   - ☐ d) Transcend

6. The Marvel character Iron Man first appeared in which comic book?

☐ a) *Amazing Adventures*

☐ b) *Tales to Astonish*

☐ c) *Strange Tales*

☐ d) *Tales of Suspense*

7. Quint Verginix is a character in which chronicles?

☐ a) *The Spiderwick Chronicles*

☐ b) *The Edge Chronicles*

☐ c) *The Chronicles of Thomas Covenant, the Unbeliever*

☐ d) *The Chronicles of Narnia*

8. Saren Arterius is a villain in which video game?

☐ a) *Mass Effect*

☐ b) *Fallout*

☐ c) *Metro 2033*

☐ d) *Resident Evil*

9. What is the name of Rachel Luttrell's character in *Stargate: Atlantis*?

☐ a) Carol Beckett

☐ b) Elizabeth Weir

☐ c) Jennifer Keller

☐ d) Teyla Emmagan

10. The island upon which *Jurassic Park* is set is closest to which country?

☐ a) Chile

☐ b) Costa Rica

☐ c) Argentina

☐ d) Mexico

QUIZ 68
GENERAL KNOWLEDGE, TRUE OR FALSE

1. Captain America first appeared in *Captain America Comics* #1.
   ☐ True   ☐ False

2. Two actors from the 1987 film *Predator* went on to become State Governors.
   ☐ True   ☐ False

3. Dr. Daniel Jackson, as portrayed by Michael Shanks, appears in four episodes of *Stargate: Universe.*
   ☐ True   ☐ False

4. DC Comics character Jonah Hex served as a Union sharpshooter during the Civil War.
   ☐ True   ☐ False

5. There was a television series based on the movie and story *Total Recall.*
   ☐ True   ☐ False

6. The majority of dinosaur species seen in the film *Jurassic Park* did NOT live in the Jurassic era.
   ☐ True   ☐ False

7. George R. R. Martin's real name is Gerald Reston Martin.
   ☐ True   ☐ False

8. The music for *The Princess Bride* was written by Mark Knopfler, lead singer of Dire Straits.
   ☐ True   ☐ False

9. The novel *The Ship of Ishtar* was written by H. Rider Haggard.
   ☐ True   ☐ False

10. The "New Wave" in science fiction began in the 1940s and '50s.
    ☐ True   ☐ False

QUIZ 69
GENERAL KNOWLEDGE QUESTIONS, SHORT ANSWER

1. Who wrote and directed the 1973 film *Westworld*?

   ....

2. Who was the first actor to portray The Master in the television series *Doctor Who*?

   ....

3. What spaceship was armed with "the wave motion gun"?

   ....

4. Who serves as Dante's guide through the Inferno?

   ....

5. The short-lived television show *The Lone Gunmen*, which debuted in 2001, was a spin-off from what other television show?

   ....

6. What is the name of the character played by James Earl Jones in the 1982 film *Conan the Barbarian*?

   ....

7. In what city would you find Arkham Asylum?

   ....

8. Who played the recurring character Autolycus, the so-called "King of Thieves" in *Xena: Warrior Princess* and *Hercules: The Legendary Journeys*?

   ....

9. Elijah Snow, Jakita Wagner, The Drummer, and Ambrose Chase are characters in what comic book?

   ....

10. The country of Panem is the setting for what trilogy of novels?

   ....

QUIZ 70
STAR WARS SPECIES, MATCH UP

Match each of these characters from the *Star Wars* films with his or her species.

1. Chewbacca

2. Greedo

3. Bib Fortuna

4. Wicket

5. Nien Nunb

6. Darth Maul

7. Admiral Ackbar

8. Bossk

9. Ki-Adi-Mundi

10. Zuckuss

a) Ewok

b) Mon Calamari

c) Sullustan

d) Trandoshan

e) Gand

f) Wookiee

g) Cerean

h) Twi'lek

i) Dathomirian Zabrak

j) Rodian

QUIZ 71
GENERAL KNOWLEDGE, MULTIPLE CHOICE

1. According to Anne Rice's novels the vampire known as Lestat was born in which year?
   - ☐ a) 1645
   - ☐ b) 1690
   - ☐ c) 1760
   - ☐ d) 1799

2. In the *Discworld* series by Terry Pratchett, what is the name of Death's horse?
   - ☐ a) Binky
   - ☐ b) Pinky
   - ☐ c) Slinky
   - ☐ d) Clyde

3. What is the subtitle of the 1987 film *Superman IV*?
   - ☐ a) *A View from Space*
   - ☐ b) *The Final Frontier*
   - ☐ c) *The Quest for Peace*
   - ☐ d) *The Man of Steel*

4. According to the *Star Trek* franchise, who was captain of the *Enterprise NX-01*?
   - ☐ a) Jonathan Archer
   - ☐ b) James T. Kirk
   - ☐ c) Jean-Luc Picard
   - ☐ d) Christopher Pike

5. Which of these mythical monsters was NOT defeated by Hercules as part of his famous labors?
   - ☐ a) The Kraken
   - ☐ b) The Lernaean Hydra
   - ☐ c) Cerberus
   - ☐ d) The Nemean Lion

6. Who was the first man to use the superhero name Green Lantern?

☐ a) Hal Jordan

☐ b) Alan Scott

☐ c) Guy Gardner

☐ d) Kyle Rayner

7. Who wrote the 1996 novel *The Reality Dysfunction*?

☐ a) Iain M. Banks

☐ b) Peter F. Hamilton

☐ c) Alastair Reynolds

☐ d) Charles Stross

8. The Marvel superhero Hawkeye was married to which superheroine?

☐ a) Black Widow

☐ b) Mockingbird

☐ c) Wasp

☐ d) Scarlet Witch

9. Who played Darth Vader in *Star Wars: A New Hope*?

☐ a) Peter Mayhew

☐ b) Anthony Daniels

☐ c) David Prowse

☐ d) Jack Purvis

10. Who directed the 1995 anime film *Ghost in the Shell*?

☐ a) Makoto Shinkai

☐ b) Hayao Miyazaki

☐ c) Katsuhiro Otomo

☐ d) Mamoru Oshii

QUIZ 72
GENERAL KNOWLEDGE, MULTIPLE CHOICE

1. In the Marvel Comics universe, how many gems are needed to complete
    the Infinity Gauntlet?
    - ☐ a) 4
    - ☐ b) 5
    - ☐ c) 6
    - ☐ d) 7

2. Which of these novels was NOT written by John Wyndham?
    - ☐ a) *The Day of the Triffids*
    - ☐ b) *The Kraken Wakes*
    - ☐ c) *Chocky*
    - ☐ d) *The Wanderer*

3. Which of these is the third of the Sookie Stackhouse novels (also known
    as *The Southern Vampire Mysteries*)?
    - ☐ a) *Dead as a Doornail*
    - ☐ b) *Dead Until Dark*
    - ☐ c) *Club Dead*
    - ☐ d) *From Dead to Worse*

4. In which film does amnesiac John Murdoch discover he has the ability
    to "tune" the world around him?
    - ☐ a) *Donnie Darko*
    - ☐ b) *Dark City*
    - ☐ c) *The Narrow Margin*
    - ☐ d) *The Groundstar Conspiracy*

5. In which of these books in *The Chronicles of Narnia* does Prince Caspian
    (later King Caspian X) NOT appear?
    - ☐ a) *The Voyage of the Dawn Treader*
    - ☐ b) *The Silver Chair*
    - ☐ c) *The Last Battle*
    - ☐ d) *The Horse and His Boy*

6. How many years separate the theatrical release of *The Return of the Jedi* and *Star Wars Episode I: The Phantom Menace?*
   - ☐ a) 9
   - ☐ b) 16
   - ☐ c) 21
   - ☐ d) 25

7. Which of these Norse gods only had one hand?
   - ☐ a) Balder
   - ☐ b) Tyr
   - ☐ c) Heimdall
   - ☐ d) Odin

8. Written by Alan Moore, the comic story, "Whatever Happened to the Man of Tomorrow?" featured which superhero?
   - ☐ a) Superman
   - ☐ b) Batman
   - ☐ c) Spider-Man
   - ☐ d) Green Lantern

9. The superhero team Alpha Flight is based in which country?
   - ☐ a) Australia
   - ☐ b) Ireland
   - ☐ c) Canada
   - ☐ d) England

10. In the *Halo* video game universe, in which year did human worlds first come under attack from the Covenant?
   - ☐ a) 2348
   - ☐ b) 2525
   - ☐ c) 2787
   - ☐ d) 2999

QUIZ 73
GENERAL KNOWLEDGE, TRUE OR FALSE

1. Jonathan Frakes made his film directorial debut on *Star Trek Generations*.
   ☐ True   ☐ False

2. King Arthur pulled Excalibur out of the stone.
   ☐ True   ☐ False

3. Kylie Minogue played the role of Cammy White in the 1994 film *Street Fighter*.
   ☐ True   ☐ False

4. Billy Dee Williams played Commissioner Gordon in the 1989 film *Batman* directed by Tim Burton.
   ☐ True   ☐ False

5. In the *War of the Worlds* television series, the alien invaders did NOT originate on Mars.
   ☐ True   ☐ False

6. Michael Shanks played the recurring role of Hawkman in the television series *Smallville*.
   ☐ True   ☐ False

7. Author Jasper Fforde has written a series of novels starring a character named Wednesday Next.
   ☐ True   ☐ False

8. The Rocketeer first appeared in a comic book called *Starslayer*.
   ☐ True   ☐ False

9. Cesar Romero played The Joker in the 1960s *Batman* television series.
   ☐ True   ☐ False

10. The anime series *Cowboy Bebop* appeared on television in America before it did in Japan.
    ☐ True   ☐ False

QUIZ 74
GENERAL KNOWLEDGE QUESTIONS, SHORT ANSWER

1. Which of the *Star Wars* cartoons, launched in 1985, produced more episodes: *Droids* or *Ewoks*?

   ....

2. What are the next two words in this song: "I want to lie, shipwrecked and comatose, drinking fresh…"?

   ....

3. In the television show *Futurama*, what is Bender's middle name?

   ....

4. What kind of blood can trolls smell in the 2010 film *Trollhunter*?

   ....

5. In the Ultimate Marvel continuum, who became Spider-Man after the death of Peter Parker?

   ....

6. In the television show *Firefly*, what is Kaylee's full name?

   ....

7. What was the title of the official *Dungeons & Dragons* magazine that focused on presenting new adventures?

   ....

8. What does B.P.R.D. stand for in the comic book of that title?

   ....

9. Which trick-shot comic book character was created first: Green Arrow or Hawkeye?

   ....

10. What is the longest-running North American science-fiction television series?

   ....

QUIZ 75
SUPERHEROES, MATCH UP

Match up these superheroes with their alter egos.

1. Black Panther

a) Remy LeBeau

2. Hawkman

b) Katar Hol

3. The Beast

c) Michael Jon Carter

4. Blade

d) Jefferson Pierce

5. Wildcat

e) Ted Grant

6. Gambit

f) Eric Brooks

7. The Rocketeer

g) T'Challa

8. Captain Britain

h) Cliff Secord

9. Black Lightning

i) Hank McCoy

10. Booster Gold

j) Brian Braddock

QUIZ 76
GENERAL KNOWLEDGE, MULTIPLE CHOICE

1. In the 1968 film *2001: A Space Odyssey*, the space craft *Discovery One* travels from Earth to which planet?
   - ☐ a) Mercury
   - ☐ b) Mars
   - ☐ c) Jupiter
   - ☐ d) Saturn

2. In *Star Wars: A New Hope*, the Battle of Yavin takes place over which planet?
   - ☐ a) Yavin 1
   - ☐ b) Yavin 2
   - ☐ c) Yavin 3
   - ☐ d) Yavin 4

3. Kilgore Trout is a fictional science-fiction writer created by which real author?
   - ☐ a) Aldous Huxley
   - ☐ b) Kurt Vonnegut
   - ☐ c) Philip José Farmer
   - ☐ d) Theodore Sturgeon

4. In *Star Trek: The Next Generation*, what race is Ensign Ro Laren?
   - ☐ a) Betazoid
   - ☐ b) Bajoran
   - ☐ c) Klingon
   - ☐ d) Vulcan

5. The British science-fiction series *The Prisoner* first aired in which year?
   - ☐ a) 1965
   - ☐ b) 1967
   - ☐ c) 1969
   - ☐ d) 1971

6. Beowulf was a member of which tribe of people?
   - ☐ a) Jutes
   - ☐ b) Geats
   - ☐ c) Danes
   - ☐ d) Swedes

7. Which of these heroes did NOT appear in the first ever issue of *The Avengers* comic?
   - ☐ a) Captain America
   - ☐ b) Iron Man
   - ☐ c) Thor
   - ☐ d) Hulk

8. Who wrote the novel *The Postman*?
   - ☐ a) David Brin
   - ☐ b) Poul Anderson
   - ☐ c) Ray Bradbury
   - ☐ d) Andre Norton

9. Which of these is NOT a member of Delta Squad in the *Gears of War* video game?
   - ☐ a) Marcus Fenix
   - ☐ b) Augustus Cole
   - ☐ c) Damon Baird
   - ☐ d) Victor Hoffman

10. How many "Light Warriors" are there in the original *Final Fantasy* video game?
    - ☐ a) 2
    - ☐ b) 4
    - ☐ c) 6
    - ☐ d) 8

QUIZ 77
GENERAL KNOWLEDGE, MULTIPLE CHOICE

1. Which of these films, released in 1973, was the fifth and final part of the original series of *Planet of the Apes* movies?
    - ☐ a) *Escape from the Planet of the Apes*
    - ☐ b) *Beneath the Planet of the Apes*
    - ☐ c) *Battle for the Planet of the Apes*
    - ☐ d) *Conquest of the Planet of the Apes*

2. Which novel won the 2013 Hugo Award?
    - ☐ a) *2312* by Kim Stanley Robinson
    - ☐ b) *Blackout* by Mira Grant
    - ☐ c) *Throne of the Crescent Moon* by Saladin Ahmed
    - ☐ d) *Redshirts* by John Scalzi

3. Which of these characters never made an appearance in *Star Trek: The Next Generation*?
    - ☐ a) Pavel Chekov
    - ☐ b) Spock
    - ☐ c) Leonard McCoy
    - ☐ d) Montgomery Scott

4. The comic book *Bone* ran for how many issues?
    - ☐ a) 55
    - ☐ b) 75
    - ☐ c) 95
    - ☐ d) 115

5. In which state was the town of Jericho in the television show of the same name?
    - ☐ a) Ohio
    - ☐ b) Nebraska
    - ☐ c) Arkansas
    - ☐ d) Kansas

6. The novel *Jonathan Strange & Mr. Norrell* by Susanna Clarke is set in which century?
   - ☐ a) 17th
   - ☐ b) 18th
   - ☐ c) 19th
   - ☐ d) 20th

7. In *The Empire Strikes Back*, which Imperial Admiral is killed by Darth Vader because he came out of hyperspace too close to the planet Hoth?
   - ☐ a) Krennel
   - ☐ b) Motti
   - ☐ c) Piett
   - ☐ d) Ozzel

8. What is the title of the first part of T. H. White's novel *The Once & Future King*?
   - ☐ a) "The Ill-Made Knight"
   - ☐ b) "The Sword in the Stone"
   - ☐ c) "The Candle in the Wind"
   - ☐ d) "The Book Merlyn"

9. The Marvel Comics villain Kingpin first appeared in which comic book?
   - ☐ a) *The Amazing Spider-Man*
   - ☐ b) *Daredevil*
   - ☐ c) *The Punisher*
   - ☐ d) *Heroes for Hire*

10. Who is the main character of the first two *Portal* video games?
   - ☐ a) Trick
   - ☐ b) Chell
   - ☐ c) Swept
   - ☐ d) Leeloo

QUIZ 78
GENERAL KNOWLEDGE, TRUE OR FALSE

1. The 1982 film *The Thing* is based on the novella "Who Goes There?" by John W. Campbell, Jr.
    ☐ True   ☐ False

2. William Moulton Marston, who created the character Wonder Woman, also invented the systolic blood pressure test, a component of the modern polygraph.
    ☐ True   ☐ False

3. The father of space opera, E. E. "Doc" Smith, was a medical doctor.
    ☐ True   ☐ False

4. Shadowcat was one of the superhero aliases used by the Marvel mutant, Kitty Pryde.
    ☐ True   ☐ False

5. Ron Perlman has never appeared in a *Star Trek* movie.
    ☐ True   ☐ False

6. In *Mystery Science Theater 3000* the main cast are trapped on a spacecraft known as *The Satellite of Love*.
    ☐ True   ☐ False

7. Neil Gaiman is the only writer, aside from J. Michael Straczynski to write an episode in the last series of *Babylon 5*.
    ☐ True   ☐ False

8. *The Lion, the Witch and the Wardrobe* was published before *The Hobbit*.
    ☐ True   ☐ False

9. The 1999 film *The Matrix* won four Academy Awards, including the award for Best Picture.
    ☐ True   ☐ False

10. The director John Carpenter is one of the principal writers for the *Falling Skies* television series.
    ☐ True   ☐ False

QUIZ 79
GENERAL KNOWLEDGE QUESTIONS, SHORT ANSWER

1. What is the full name of "UU," the school of wizardry in Terry Pratchett's *Discworld* series?

   ....

2. What was the name of Walter Koenig's character in the television series *Babylon 5*?

   ....

HARD

3. What was the title of the short-lived science-fiction western television series that aired in 1995 and starred Richard Dean Anderson?

   ....

4. What actor portrayed Dr. Who in the films *Dr. Who and the Daleks* and *Daleks – Invasion Earth 2150 A.D.*?

   ....

5. Who played the character of Professor Maximillian Arturo in the television show *Sliders*?

   ....

6. Who was the mother of Sleipnir, the eight-legged horse of the Norse god Odin?

   ....

7. Author Suzanne Collins drew inspiration from the myth of which Ancient Greek hero in writing *The Hunger Games*?

   ....

8. Which science-fiction author is acknowledged in the end credits of *The Terminator* as being an influence on the movie following a lawsuit?

   ....

9. What company developed the original *Doom* video game?

   ....

10. What term is used to describe the practice of acquiring treasure in online games for the purposes of selling it for real-world currency?

   ....

QUIZ 80
ACTORS, MATCH UP

Match these television characters to the actor who portrayed them.

1. Ka D'Argo   a) Terry O'Quinn

2. Charles "Trip" Tucker III   b) Craig Charles

3. Capt. Dylan Hunt   c) Anthony Simcoe

4. Roj Blake   d) Ron Glass

5. John Doggett   e) Robert Patrick

6. John Locke   f) Connor Trinneer

7. Michael Garibaldi   g) Jerry Doyle

8. Dave Lister   h) Jason Momoa

9. Ronon Dex   i) Gareth Thomas

10. Derrial Book   j) Kevin Sorbo

QUIZ 81
GENERAL KNOWLEDGE, MULTIPLE CHOICE

1. The "Known Space" universe was invented by which author?
   - ☐ a) Isaac Asimov
   - ☐ b) Larry Niven
   - ☐ c) Arthur C. Clarke
   - ☐ d) Greg Bear

2. According to Philip Pullman's *His Dark Materials* trilogy, protagonist Lyra Belacqua is brought up in which Oxford College?
   - ☐ a) Jordan
   - ☐ b) Nuffield
   - ☐ c) Wolfson
   - ☐ d) Linacre

3. According to Greek myth, what was the name of Heracles' twin brother?
   - ☐ a) Iolaus
   - ☐ b) Hylas
   - ☐ c) Eurystheus
   - ☐ d) Iphicles

4. The character Buck Rogers first appeared in which media?
   - ☐ a) radio serial
   - ☐ b) pulp magazine
   - ☐ c) comic book
   - ☐ d) movie serial

5. The controversial comic character "Ebony White" was an occasional sidekick to which hero?
   - ☐ a) Batman
   - ☐ b) The Spirit
   - ☐ c) The Phantom
   - ☐ d) Captain America

6. Who wrote the novel *Shadowmarch*?
   - ☐ a) Susan Cooper
   - ☐ b) N. K. Jemisin
   - ☐ c) Tad Williams
   - ☐ d) William Horwood

7. What is the main occupation of Samus Aran, the protagonist of the *Metroid* series of video games?
   - ☐ a) Space Police Officer
   - ☐ b) Pirate
   - ☐ c) Bounty Hunter
   - ☐ d) Archaeologist

8. What was the last novel of *The Chronicles of Narnia* to be published?
   - ☐ a) *The Last Battle*
   - ☐ b) *The Magician's Nephew*
   - ☐ c) *The Horse and His Boy*
   - ☐ d) *The Silver Chair*

9. What is the Japanese name for Godzilla?
   - ☐ a) Godzilla
   - ☐ b) Gojira
   - ☐ c) Kaiju
   - ☐ d) Ishirō

10. Which of these was NOT a playable character in the 1985 arcade game *Gauntlet*?
    - ☐ a) Wizard
    - ☐ b) Elf
    - ☐ c) Dwarf
    - ☐ d) Valkyrie

QUIZ 82
GENERAL KNOWLEDGE, MULTIPLE CHOICE

1. Which barbarian from fantasy literature carries a sword named "Graywand"?
   - ☐ a) Conan
   - ☐ b) Throngor
   - ☐ c) Brak
   - ☐ d) Fafhrd

2. In which film was the hero nearly killed "...a million miles from nowhere with a gung-ho iguana"?
   - ☐ a) *The Last Starfighter*
   - ☐ b) *Enemy Mine*
   - ☐ c) *Wing Commander*
   - ☐ d) *Return of the Jedi*

3. Which incarnation of The Flash died during the *Crisis on Infinite Earths*?
   - ☐ a) Jay Garrick
   - ☐ b) Wally West
   - ☐ c) Barry Allen
   - ☐ d) Bart Allen

4. In Robert A. Heinlein's novel *Stranger in a Strange Land*, on which planet is the protagonist Valentine Michael Smith born?
   - ☐ a) Earth
   - ☐ b) Mercury
   - ☐ c) Venus
   - ☐ d) Mars

5. Which comic book company first had the license to publish *Star Wars* comics?
   - ☐ a) Marvel
   - ☐ b) DC
   - ☐ c) Dark Horse
   - ☐ d) Archie Comics

HARD

6. Which legendary hero slew the dragon Fafnir?

☐ a) St. George

☐ b) Beowulf

☐ c) Sigurd

☐ d) Lancelot

7. What name is given to the aliens in both the film and television show *Alien Nation*?

☐ a) Visitors

☐ b) Newcomers

☐ c) Bemmies

☐ d) Spottie

8. In Spider-Man comics, which supervillain's real name is Adrian Toomes?

☐ a) Electro

☐ b) Doctor Octopus

☐ c) Vulture

☐ d) Shocker

9. Who played The Flash in the 1990 television series of the same title?

☐ a) Alex Désert

☐ b) Danny Bilson

☐ c) Paul De Meo

☐ d) John Wesley Shipp

10. Who wrote the novel *Mythago Wood*?

☐ a) Robin Hobb

☐ b) Robert Holdstock

☐ c) Joe Abercrombie

☐ d) Neil Gaiman

QUIZ 83
GENERAL KNOWLEDGE, TRUE OR FALSE

1. Spider Jerusalem is the main character of a comic book series called *Nanocity*.
   ☐ True ☐ False

2. According to *Star Trek: The Next Generation*, the young Jean-Luc Picard failed his Starfleet Academy entrance exam three times before being admitted.
   ☐ True ☐ False

3. Reese Witherspoon played Batgirl in the 1997 film *Batman and Robin*.
   ☐ True ☐ False

4. *The NeverEnding Story* was actually less than two hours long.
   ☐ True ☐ False

5. John Williams composed the scores for all of the following movies: *Jaws*, *Star Wars: A New Hope*, *E.T. the Extra-Terrestrial*, *Superman*, *Raiders of the Lost Ark*, and *Harry Potter and the Philosopher's Stone*.
   ☐ True ☐ False

6. Aquaman was part of the very first adventure of the Justice League of America.
   ☐ True ☐ False

7. The main character in the original *Zork* video game is named "Lothar."
   ☐ True ☐ False

8. The novel *Harry Potter and the Philospher's Stone* was first published in 1994.
   ☐ True ☐ False

9. Madame Tussauds in Las Vegas includes a wax statue of Master Chief from the video game *Halo*.
   ☐ True ☐ False

10. J. R. R. Tolkien spent more than 20 years writing *The Lord of the Rings*.
    ☐ True ☐ False

QUIZ 84
GENERAL KNOWLEDGE QUESTIONS, SHORT ANSWER

1. According to the *A Song of Ice and Fire* series, "dragonglass" is the Westeros name for what real-world material that can be fashioned into weapons capable of killing the White Walkers?

   ....

2. Who was the writer and illustrator of the comic book series *Bone*?

   ....

3. Who founded the GenCon gaming convention?

   ....

4. What was the first novel to win the science-fiction "triple-crown" that is the Nebula, the Hugo, and the Philip K. Dick Awards?

   ....

5. What actor portrayed Julius Caesar in the television show *Xena: Warrior Princess*?

   ....

6. What famous puppeteer animated and provided the voice for Yoda in *The Empire Strikes Back*?

   ....

7. Which *Doctor Who* spin-off show ran for more seasons: *Torchwood* or *The Sarah Jane Adventures*?

   ....

8. In the science-fiction mini-series *V*, what was "V" short for?

   ....

9. Max Headroom served as a spokesman for which soft drink: Coke or Pepsi?

   ....

10. According to the comics, what does Hellboy smell like?

   ....

QUIZ 85
MOVIE QUOTES, MATCH UP

Match up these movie quotes with the film in which they appear.

1. "Hokey religions and ancient weapons are no match for a good blaster at your side, kid."

   a) *Stargate*

2. "You know the saying, 'Human see, human do'."

   b) *The Terminator*

3. "Come with me if you want to live."

   c) *Predator*

4. "Have fun storming the castle!"

   d) *Star Wars: A New Hope*

5. "It means buckle your seatbelt, Dorothy, 'cause Kansas is going bye-bye."

   e) *Blade Runner*

6. "Give my regards to King Tut, asshole."

   f) *The Matrix*

7. "If it bleeds, we can kill it."

   g) *Mars Attacks!*

8. "Listen lady, I only speak two languages: English and bad English."

   h) *The Princess Bride*

9. "The light that burns twice as bright burns half as long...and you have burned so very, very brightly, Roy."

   i) *Planet of the Apes*

10. "ack, ack, ack."

    j) *The Fifth Element*

QUIZ 86
GENERAL KNOWLEDGE, MULTIPLE CHOICE

1. In which year was George Orwell's *1984* first published?
   - ☐ a) 1949
   - ☐ b) 1954
   - ☐ c) 1959
   - ☐ d) 1964

2. Who was the first leader of the West Coast Avengers?
   - ☐ a) Iron Man
   - ☐ b) Hawkeye
   - ☐ c) Wonder Man
   - ☐ d) Black Widow

3. Who directed the 1988 anime film *Akira*?
   - ☐ a) Takeshi Seyama
   - ☐ b) Mitsuo Iwata
   - ☐ c) Tarō Ishida
   - ☐ d) Katsuhiro Otomo

4. In 1967, Samuel R. Delany's novel *Babel-17* was awarded a joint Nebula Award with which other novel?
   - ☐ a) *The Dispossessed* by Ursula K. Le Guin
   - ☐ b) *Flowers for Algernon* by Daniel Keyes
   - ☐ c) *The Claw of the Conciliator* by Gene Wolfe
   - ☐ d) *Startide Rising* by David Brin

5. What was the birth name of the Minotaur, the mythical creature slain by Theseus in the Labyrinth?
   - ☐ a) Cimon
   - ☐ b) Asterion
   - ☐ c) Procrustes
   - ☐ d) Sciron

6. In the Marvel universe, James Rupert "Rhodey" Rhodes sometimes takes on the mantle of which superhero?

☐ a) War Machine

☐ b) Power Man

☐ c) Black Panther

☐ d) Falcon

7. Which of the *Lensman* novels did E. E. "Doc" Smith write first?

☐ a) *Triplanetary*

☐ b) *First Lensman*

☐ c) *Galactic Patrol*

☐ d) *Gray Lensman*

8. What was Andre Norton's actual first name?

☐ a) Alice

☐ b) Belle

☐ c) Catherine

☐ d) Dorothy

9. Which of these actresses did NOT play Catwoman opposite Adam West as Batman?

☐ a) Jean Harlow

☐ b) Julie Newmar

☐ c) Lee Meriwether

☐ d) Eartha Kitt

10. The body-swapping killer Dog-Face Joe appears in which Tim Powers novel?

☐ a) *The Drawing of the Dark*

☐ b) *The Anubis Gates*

☐ c) *On Stranger Tides*

☐ d) *Dinner at Deviant's Palace*

QUIZ 87
GENERAL KNOWLEDGE, MULTIPLE CHOICE

1. According to J. R. R. Tolkien's *The Lord of the Rings*, which of these is NOT another name given to Aragorn?
    ☐ a) Wingfoot
    ☐ b) Thorongil
    ☐ c) Elessar
    ☐ d) Eldakar

2. In *Return of the Jedi*, what was the name of the Ewok chief who aided the Rebel Alliance against Imperial Forces on the forest moon of Endor?
    ☐ a) Ra-Lee
    ☐ b) Chirpa
    ☐ c) Bozzie
    ☐ d) Paploo

3. Which of these is NOT one of the great houses in the BattleTech universe?
    ☐ a) Steiner
    ☐ b) Kurita
    ☐ c) Carpathia
    ☐ d) Liao

4. In which year was *Twilight Zone: The Movie* released?
    ☐ a) 1968
    ☐ b) 1974
    ☐ c) 1978
    ☐ d) 1983

5. Which of these books is NOT part of Isaac Asimov's *Foundation* series?
    ☐ a) *Forward the Foundation*
    ☐ b) *Foundation's Edge*
    ☐ c) *Foundation and Earth*
    ☐ d) *Foundation Falls*

6. Which television program followed the adventures of the Blackwood Project?
   - ☐ a) *Caprica*
   - ☐ b) *The Six Million Dollar Man*
   - ☐ c) *War of the Worlds*
   - ☐ d) *Dark Angel*

7. According to the *New 52*, who is Wonder Woman's father?
   - ☐ a) Zeus
   - ☐ b) Ares
   - ☐ c) Apollo
   - ☐ d) Hercules

8. The name of which kitchen utensil serves as the battle cry for the superhero The Tick?
   - ☐ a) fork
   - ☐ b) spoon
   - ☐ c) spatula
   - ☐ d) whisk

9. The Black Mesa Research Facility is the main setting of which video game?
   - ☐ a) *Fallout*
   - ☐ b) *Resident Evil*
   - ☐ c) *Half-Life*
   - ☐ d) *BioShock*

10. The 1981 film *Outland* is set on which moon of Jupiter?
    - ☐ a) Callisto
    - ☐ b) Ganymede
    - ☐ c) Europa
    - ☐ d) Io

QUIZ 88
GENERAL KNOWLEDGE, TRUE OR FALSE

1. *A Wrinkle in Time* by Madeleine L'Engle opens with, "It was a dark and stormy night…"
   ☐ True   ☐ False

2. The comic character Miyamoto Usagi first appeared in *The Teenage Mutant Ninja Turtles*.
   ☐ True   ☐ False

3. Liam Neeson plays Lancelot in the 1981 film *Excalibur*.
   ☐ True   ☐ False

4. *The Hunger Games* appeared on the *New York Times* Best Seller List for over 100 consecutive weeks.
   ☐ True   ☐ False

5. Patrick Troughton, the second actor to portray the Doctor in *Doctor Who*, was also the first actor to portray Robin Hood in a television series.
   ☐ True   ☐ False

6. Sean Pertwee appears in all of the following movies: *Dog Soldiers*, *Soldier*, *Event Horizon*, and *Mutant Chronicles*.
   ☐ True   ☐ False

7. *The Princess Bride* was mostly filmed in New Zealand.
   ☐ True   ☐ False

8. Bender in *Futurama* and Marcus Fenix in the video game *Gears of War* have the same voice actor.
   ☐ True   ☐ False

9. In older tradition a "jack-o'-lantern" and a "will-o'-the-wisp" are the same thing.
   ☐ True   ☐ False

10. A live-action film based on Anne McCaffrey's *Pern* novels has never been produced.
    ☐ True   ☐ False

QUIZ 89
GENERAL KNOWLEDGE QUESTIONS, SHORT ANSWER

1. What was the birth name of comic book legend Stan Lee?

....

2. What movie features characters named Randall, Fidgit, Strutter, Og, Wally, and Vermin?

....

3. Complete this phrase: "Who knows what evil lurks in the hearts of men?..."

....

4. Who directed the 2003 film *Daredevil*?

....

5. What author came up with the concept of the "Wold Newton Family"?

....

6. What are the symbols on the stargate called?

....

7. Richard Bachman is a pen name for what writer?

....

8. *Pawn of Prophecy, Demon Lord of Karanda*, and *Seeress of Kell* are all fantasy novels by what author?

....

9. The comic book *Fray* is a futuristic spin-off from what television series?

....

10. In the *A Song of Ice and Fire* series, which of the great houses of the Seven Kingdoms has its seat at Riverrun?

....

QUIZ 90
ACTORS IN *LOST*, MATCH UP

Match up these actors from the television series *Lost* with the television series or movie in which they appeared.

1. Terry O'Quinn

2. Evangeline Lilly

3. Daniel Dae Kim

4. Maggie Grace

5. Naveen Andrews

6. Dominic Monaghan

7. Harold Perrineau

8. Michelle Rodriguez

9. Mira Furlan

10. Ian Somerhalder

a) *Lockout*

b) *Babylon 5: Crusade*

c) *Avatar*

d) *The Lord of the Rings: The Fellowship of the Ring*

e) *Constantine*

f) *Millennium*

g) *The Vampire Diaries*

h) *Babylon 5*

i) *The Hobbit: The Desolation of Smaug*

j) *Once Upon a Time in Wonderland*

QUIZ 91
GENERAL KNOWLEDGE, MULTIPLE CHOICE

1. Who was the first actress to play the role of Saavik in the *Star Trek* films?
   - ☐ a) Robin Curtis
   - ☐ b) Nichelle Nichols
   - ☐ c) Kirstie Alley
   - ☐ d) Majel Barrett

2. In the novel *Among Others* by Jo Walton, diary writer and fantasy fan Mori is from which part of the British Isles?
   - ☐ a) The Isle of Wight
   - ☐ b) The Orkneys
   - ☐ c) The Isle of Man
   - ☐ d) Wales

3. What is Max's last name in the *Mad Max* series of films?
   - ☐ a) Rockatansky
   - ☐ b) Bellamy
   - ☐ c) Hudson
   - ☐ d) Wochowski

4. Which band makes an appearance in *Back to the Future: Part III*?
   - ☐ a) Bon Jovi
   - ☐ b) ZZ Top
   - ☐ c) Huey Lewis and the News
   - ☐ d) Mike and the Mechanics

5. In *Akira*, what is the name of Shotaro Kaneda's biker gang?
   - ☐ a) The Clowns
   - ☐ b) The Bin-Liners
   - ☐ c) The Needles
   - ☐ d) The Capsules

6. Winry Rockbell is a character in which anime series?

☐ a) *Last Exile*

☐ b) *Full Metal Alchemist*

☐ c) *Neon Genesis Evangelion*

☐ d) *Cowboy Bebop*

7. What was the subtitle for the third *Dungeons & Dragons* movie?

☐ a) *The Book of Vile Darkness*

☐ b) *Wrath of the Dragon God*

☐ c) *Return to the Abyss*

☐ d) *Forgotten Realms*

8. Who wrote the story "The King of the Golden River"?

☐ a) Charles Dickens

☐ b) George MacDonald

☐ c) William Makepeace Thackeray

☐ d) John Ruskin

9. What was the first novel to feature Karl Edward Wagner's character Kane, The Mystic Swordsman?

☐ a) *Dark Crusade*

☐ b) *Night Winds*

☐ c) *Bloodstone*

☐ d) *Gods in Darkness*

10. Which brand of beer does E.T. drink?

☐ a) Budweiser

☐ b) Miller

☐ c) Coors

☐ d) Michelob

QUIZ 92
GENERAL KNOWLEDGE, MULTIPLE CHOICE

1. Which 1956 science-fiction novel was originally published in Britain
    with the title *Tiger! Tiger!*
    ☐ a) *I, Robot*
    ☐ b) *The Moon is a Harsh Mistress*
    ☐ c) *The Stars My Destination*
    ☐ d) *Childhood's End*

2. What is the name of the comic book store in *The Simpsons*?
    ☐ a) The Robot Factory
    ☐ b) The Dungeon Master
    ☐ c) The Android's Dungeon
    ☐ d) Dream Wizards

3. According to *The X-Files*, how old was Fox Mulder when his sister was
    abducted by aliens?
    ☐ a) 6
    ☐ b) 12
    ☐ c) 17
    ☐ d) 22

4. In *Star Trek: Deep Space Nine*, what is station commander Benjamin
    Sisko's middle name?
    ☐ a) Lafayette
    ☐ b) Joseph
    ☐ c) Tecumseh
    ☐ d) William

5. Who was the first official leader of the Marvel superhero team, *Force Works*?
    ☐ a) Scarlet Witch
    ☐ b) Iron Man
    ☐ c) U.S. Agent
    ☐ d) Spider-Woman

6. What nationality was the horror and science-fiction author, William Hope Hodgson?

☐ a) American

☐ b) English

☐ c) Irish

☐ d) Canadian

7. The character Molly Millions, who first appeared in William Gibson's novel *Neuromancer*, reappeared in his later novel, *Mona Lisa Overdrive*, under which new alias?

☐ a) Sister Scissor

☐ b) Razor Ra

☐ c) Beatrice Blade

☐ d) Sally Shears

8. Who wrote the post-apocalyptic novel *Swan Song*?

☐ a) C. Robert Cargill

☐ b) Lou Morgan

☐ c) Darren Shan

☐ d) Robert R. McCammon

9. In the *Anita Blake: Vampire Hunter* series, which character is NOT part of the Triumvirate?

☐ a) Anita Blake

☐ b) Jean-Claude

☐ c) Rudolph Storr

☐ d) Richard Zeeman

10. What was the title of the first *Dragonlance* novel?

☐ a) *Dragons of Autumn Twilight*

☐ b) *Dragons of Summer Flame*

☐ c) *The Nightmare Lands*

☐ d) *The Medusa Plague*

QUIZ 93
GENERAL KNOWLEDGE, TRUE OR FALSE

1. In 1966 the one-time Hugo Award for Best All-Time Series was presented to E. E. "Doc" Smith's *Lensman* series.
   ☐ True   ☐ False

2. Neil Gaiman is a quarter Cherokee.
   ☐ True   ☐ False

3. Only six episodes of the *Max Headroom* television series were ever produced.
   ☐ True   ☐ False

4. The video game *Golden Axe* features a barbarian hero named Ax Battler and a dwarf named Gilius Thunderhead.
   ☐ True   ☐ False

5. Actor Jonathan Frakes, who played William Riker in *Star Trek: The Next Generation*, also appeared in at least one episode of *Star Trek: Deep Space Nine*, *Star Trek: Voyager*, and *Star Trek: Enterprise*.
   ☐ True   ☐ False

6. The television series *Red Dwarf* was based on a radio series called *Dave Hollins: Space Cadet*.
   ☐ True   ☐ False

7. The Japanese title of *Ghost in the Shell* literally translates to "God in the Machine."
   ☐ True   ☐ False

8. George R. R. Martin wrote a novel about a band called Nazgûl.
   ☐ True   ☐ False

9. Snake Plissken was a soldier in World War III.
   ☐ True   ☐ False

10. At one point Zaphod Beeblebrox had three heads, but one committed suicide.
    ☐ True   ☐ False

QUIZ 94
GENERAL KNOWLEDGE QUESTIONS, SHORT ANSWER

1. The 1981 film, *Escape from New York* is set in what year?

   ....

2. Steve Jackson's GURPS is an acronym for what?

   ....

3. What was the full title of the second made-for-television *Ewoks* film?

   ....

4. Who played Buffy Summers in the 1992 film *Buffy the Vampire Slayer*?

   ....

5. The 1988 film *Akira* is set in what city?

   ....

6. According to Norse mythology, who lived in Nidavellir?

   ....

7. The comic character, The Crow, first appeared in comics from what publisher?

   ....

8. "Zmey," "zmiy," and "zmaj" are Slavic words for what type of legendary creature?

   ....

9. Who was the first woman to win a Hugo or Nebula Award for fiction?

   ....

10. Before the rise of the term "anime" what term was generally used in English-speaking countries to describe animated cartoons imported from Japan?

    ....

QUIZ 95
FAMOUS STEEDS, MATCH UP

Match up these riders with their horses.

1. Sandor Clegane

a) Gunpowder

2. Gandalf

b) Gringolet

3. Roland Deschain

c) Faran

4. Xena, Warrior Princess

d) Comet

5. Sparhawk

e) Rusher

6. Gawain

f) Stranger

7. Ichabod Crane

g) Asfaloth

8. Odin

h) Sleipnir

9. Brisco County, Jr.

i) Shadowfax

10. Glorfindel

j) Argo

QUIZ 96
GENERAL KNOWLEDGE, MULTIPLE CHOICE

1. Which of these is NOT one of Roger Zelazny's *Nine Princes in Amber*?
   - ☐ a) Corwin
   - ☐ b) Random
   - ☐ c) Oberon
   - ☐ d) Eric

2. The physics of which television science-fiction universe include the "Blinovitch Limitation Effect"?
   - ☐ a) *Sliders*
   - ☐ b) *Stargate*
   - ☐ c) *Quantum Leap*
   - ☐ d) *Doctor Who*

3. In the *Star Trek* franchise, what is the birth name of the character Seven of Nine?
   - ☐ a) Andrea Martin
   - ☐ b) Jeri Ryan
   - ☐ c) Annika Hansen
   - ☐ d) Camille Saviola

4. Which of these is NOT a regular member of the *Knights of the Dinner Table*?
   - ☐ a) B. A. Felton
   - ☐ b) Bob Herzog
   - ☐ c) Brian VanHoose
   - ☐ d) Nitro Ferguson

5. Which author is generally credited with coining the term "steampunk"?
   - ☐ a) James Blaylock
   - ☐ b) Tim Powers
   - ☐ c) K. W. Jeter
   - ☐ d) Keith Laumer

6. How many episodes made up the original series of *The Bubblegum Crisis*?
    - ☐ a) 8
    - ☐ b) 16
    - ☐ c) 24
    - ☐ d) 32

7. Which of these actors is NOT in the 1982 film *The Beastmaster*?
    - ☐ a) Kurt Russell
    - ☐ b) Tanya Roberts
    - ☐ c) Marc Singer
    - ☐ d) Rip Torn

8. *The Hobbit: An Unexpected Journey* became the first major film released with a rate of how many frames per second?
    - ☐ a) 24
    - ☐ b) 48
    - ☐ c) 72
    - ☐ d) 98

9. Who wrote *The Narrative of Arthur Gordon Pym of Nantucket*?
    - ☐ a) Edgar Allan Poe
    - ☐ b) Robert Louis Stevenson
    - ☐ c) Arthur Conan Doyle
    - ☐ d) Bram Stoker

10. Who created the television show *Heroes*?
    - ☐ a) Jeffery Boam
    - ☐ b) David Anders
    - ☐ c) J. J. Abrams
    - ☐ d) Tim Kring

QUIZ 97
GENERAL KNOWLEDGE, MULTIPLE CHOICE

1. The character Halrloprillalar Hotrufan first appears in which Nebula Award-winning science-fiction novel?
    - [ ] a) *Rendezvous with Rama*
    - [ ] b) *Gateway*
    - [ ] c) *Ringworld*
    - [ ] d) *A Time of Changes*

2. The 1997 animated film *Princess Mononoke* is set in which period of Japanese history?
    - [ ] a) Muromachi
    - [ ] b) Edo
    - [ ] c) Meiji
    - [ ] d) Heisei

3. According to the television series, where was Xena, Warrior Princess, born?
    - [ ] a) Delphi
    - [ ] b) Cirra
    - [ ] c) Potidaea
    - [ ] d) Amphipolis

4. The Asanbosam (or Sasabonsam) are vampire-like creatures from which part of the world?
    - [ ] a) South America
    - [ ] b) West Africa
    - [ ] c) South Africa
    - [ ] d) Oceania

5. Which of these superheroes did NOT appear in *Marvel Comics* #1?
    - [ ] a) The Sub-Mariner
    - [ ] b) The Human Torch
    - [ ] c) The Angel
    - [ ] d) Silver Surfer

6. In which year was the role-playing game *Deadlands* first released?
   - ☐ a) 1990
   - ☐ b) 1996
   - ☐ c) 2000
   - ☐ d) 2004

7. Which of these actors stars in the film *Gattaca*?
   - ☐ a) Heath Ledger
   - ☐ b) River Phoenix
   - ☐ c) Joseph Fiennes
   - ☐ d) Ethan Hawke

8. Who did Ursula K. Le Guin describe as the "First Terrible Fate that Awaiteth Unwary Beginners in Fantasy"?
   - ☐ a) H. P. Lovecraft
   - ☐ b) William Makepeace Thackeray
   - ☐ c) Lord Dunsany
   - ☐ d) J. R. R. Tolkien

9. Who founded the magazine *Amazing Stories*?
   - ☐ a) Hugo Gernsback
   - ☐ b) John Campbell
   - ☐ c) Bernarr Macfadden
   - ☐ d) Paul W. Fairman

10. Which tale comes first in Dan Simmons' novel *Hyperion*?
   - ☐ a) The Soldier's Tale
   - ☐ b) The Priest's Tale
   - ☐ c) The Poet's Tale
   - ☐ d) The Scholar's Tale

QUIZ 98
GENERAL KNOWLEDGE, TRUE OR FALSE

1. Billy Dee Williams provides the voice of LEGO figure Lando Calrissian in *The LEGO Movie*.
   ☐ True   ☐ False

2. The same man wrote the screenplays for *Ladyhawke*, *Blade Runner*, and *12 Monkeys*.
   ☐ True   ☐ False

3. Andreas Katsulas, who played G'Kar in *Babylon 5*, also had a recurring role in *Star Trek: The Next Generation*.
   ☐ True   ☐ False

4. Daniel Craig starred in a low-budget science-fiction film entitled *Cyborg Spy*.
   ☐ True   ☐ False

5. Mark Hamill, Brent Spiner, and Richard Dean Anderson have all voiced the character of the Joker in various animated Batman film and television series.
   ☐ True   ☐ False

6. No novel written by Tim Powers has ever won a Hugo or Nebula Award.
   ☐ True   ☐ False

7. The first magazine dedicated to the publication of fantasy stories was German.
   ☐ True   ☐ False

8. The 1979 film *Time After Time* tells the adventures of Jules Verne and his time machine.
   ☐ True   ☐ False

9. American playwright Tennessee Williams had a story published in *Weird Tales* magazine.
   ☐ True   ☐ False

10. According to the novel *World War Z*, the papacy relocated to Malta during the zombie wars.
    ☐ True   ☐ False

QUIZ 99
GENERAL KNOWLEDGE QUESTIONS, SHORT ANSWER

1. What famous science-fiction film was produced under the title *Blue Harvest: Horror Beyond Imagination* in order to preserve secrecy?

   ....

2. What is the English translation of *Chappa'ai*?

   ....

3. In Frank Herbert's *Dune*, House Corrino's loyal Sardaukar shock troops are trained on what planet?

   ....

4. Baba Yaga's hut has what kind of legs?

   ....

5. What type of alien monster was once described as "little green blobs in bonded polycarbide armor"?

   ....

6. Who wrote and directed the 1965 science-fiction film *Alphaville*?

   ....

7. In what 1990 film did Dylan McDermott play Moses "Hard Mo" Baxter?

   ....

8. Who created the occult detective Jules de Grandin?

   ....

9. Who wrote and performed the song *Ghostbusters* which served as the theme to the film of the same name?

   ....

10. What 2007 movie starring Jason Statham carried the subtitle *A Dungeon Siege Tale*?

   ....

QUIZ 100
MYTHOS TOMES, MATCH UP

Match up these Mythos tomes with their creators.

1. *De Vermis Mysteriis*

a) Brian Lumley

2. *The Last Revelation of Gla'aki*

b) Richard F. Searight

3. *The King in Yellow*

c) H. P. Lovecraft

4. *The Book of Iod*

d) Ramsey Campbell

5. *The Celaeno Fragments*

e) Robert E. Howard

6. *The Book of Eibon*

f) Clark Ashton Smith

7. *G'harne Fragments*

g) Henry Kuttner

8. *Unaussprechlichen Kulten*

h) Robert Bloch

9. *Eltdown Shards*

i) August Derleth

10. *Necronomicon*

j) Robert W. Chambers

QUIZ 101
GENERAL KNOWLEDGE, MULTIPLE CHOICE

1. Which season of *Star Trek: The Next Generation* contains only 22 episodes and not the usual 26?
   ☐ a) First
   ☐ b) Second
   ☐ c) Sixth
   ☐ d) Seventh

2. Who was the first actor to portray Batman on screen?
   ☐ a) Robert Lowery
   ☐ b) Adam West
   ☐ c) Lewis Wilson
   ☐ d) Kevin Conroy

3. In 1997, the DC Comics character Hawkman became a promoter of which candy bar?
   ☐ a) Baby Ruth
   ☐ b) Butterfinger
   ☐ c) Almond Joy
   ☐ d) Mars Bar

4. What was the last of the Oz books written by L. Frank Baum?
   ☐ a) *The Patchwork Girl of Oz*
   ☐ b) *The Lost Princess of Oz*
   ☐ c) *The Magic of Oz*
   ☐ d) *Glinda of Oz*

5. What is the name of the strike carrier which serves as the base of the main character in the original *Wing Commander* video game?
   ☐ a) *Tiger's Claw*
   ☐ b) *Bear Claw*
   ☐ c) *Serpent's Fang*
   ☐ d) *Eagle's Talon*

6. Which online role-playing game saw a massive outbreak of "Corrupted Blood" plague?
   - ☐ a) *Neverwinter Nights*
   - ☐ b) *Final Fantasy*
   - ☐ c) *EverQuest*
   - ☐ d) *World of Warcraft*

7. What is the name of the main character's spaceship in the anime *Planetes*?
   - ☐ a) *Fist*
   - ☐ b) *Dead Robot*
   - ☐ c) *Toy Box*
   - ☐ d) *Cutty Lark*

8. Who created the character Ferdinand Feghoot?
   - ☐ a) John Brunner
   - ☐ b) E. Nelson Bridwell
   - ☐ c) F. M. Busby
   - ☐ d) Reginald Bretnor

9. Who designed the vigilante costume worn by Stephen Amell in the television series *Arrow*?
   - ☐ a) Mark Pedowitz
   - ☐ b) Danielle Panabaker
   - ☐ c) Blake Neely
   - ☐ d) Colleen Atwood

10. Which season of *Heroes* has the fewest episodes?
   - ☐ a) 2
   - ☐ b) 3
   - ☐ c) 4
   - ☐ d) 5

HARD

QUIZ 102
GENERAL KNOWLEDGE, MULTIPLE CHOICE

1. What is the name of the concept album written by L. Ron Hubbard to serve as a soundtrack to his novel *Battlefield Earth*?
   - ☐ a) *Space Fight*
   - ☐ b) *Space Jazz*
   - ☐ c) *Space Rock*
   - ☐ d) *Space Strings*

2. According to the *Star Trek* universe, which of these is a rank in the Cardassian military?
   - ☐ a) Gul
   - ☐ b) Dal
   - ☐ c) Gil
   - ☐ d) Gor

3. According to Frankish legend, what is the name of Roland's sword?
   - ☐ a) Joyeuse
   - ☐ b) Durendal
   - ☐ c) Hauteclere
   - ☐ d) Almace

4. "Project Tic-Toc" is the name of a US Government program devoted to time travel in which television series?
   - ☐ a) *Continuum*
   - ☐ b) *Voyages*
   - ☐ c) *Quantum Leap*
   - ☐ d) *The Time Tunnel*

5. In Quenyan what does the word *Úlari* mean?
   - ☐ a) Elves
   - ☐ b) Orcs
   - ☐ c) Nazgûl
   - ☐ d) Dwarves

6. Which actor read the American editions of the Harry Potter audio books?
   - ☐ a) Stephen Fry
   - ☐ b) Jim Dale
   - ☐ c) Alan Rickman
   - ☐ d) Maggie Smith

7. S. T. Joshi is a literary critic most famous for his work on which writer?
   - ☐ a) J. R. R. Tolkien
   - ☐ b) Robert E. Howard
   - ☐ c) H. P. Lovecraft
   - ☐ d) George R. R. Martin

8. Who directed the film *Dungeons & Dragons*, released in 2000?
   - ☐ a) Courtney Solomon
   - ☐ b) Jeff Preiss
   - ☐ c) Marek Kanievska
   - ☐ d) Topper Lilien

9. Which of these is NOT an executive producer on the *Game of Thrones* television series?
   - ☐ a) D. B. Weiss
   - ☐ b) Frank Doelger
   - ☐ c) Katie Weiland
   - ☐ d) George R. R. Martin

10. The *Akallabêth* is which part of the five parts of *The Silmarillion*?
   - ☐ a) first
   - ☐ b) second
   - ☐ c) third
   - ☐ d) fourth

QUIZ 103
GENERAL KNOWLEDGE, MULTIPLE CHOICE

1. Who provided the narration for the 2002 revival of *The Twilight Zone* television series?
   - ☐ a) John Travolta
   - ☐ b) Rod Serling
   - ☐ c) Leonard Nimoy
   - ☐ d) Forest Whitaker

2. In which "age" are the games *Ultima I* through *Ultima III* set?
   - ☐ a) Age of Darkness
   - ☐ b) Age of Enlightenment
   - ☐ c) Age of Armageddon
   - ☐ d) Age of Rebuilding

3. In which of these novels would you find the character Gully Foyle?
   - ☐ a) *The Forever War*
   - ☐ b) *The Stars My Destination*
   - ☐ c) *Starship Troopers*
   - ☐ d) *Childhood's End*

4. In which year was the 2012 television show *Revolution* set?
   - ☐ a) 2001
   - ☐ b) 2027
   - ☐ c) 2089
   - ☐ d) 2121

5. Who co-wrote the screenplay for *Back to the Future II* along with Robert Zemeckis?
   - ☐ a) Arthur Schmidt
   - ☐ b) Dean Cundey
   - ☐ c) Bob Gale
   - ☐ d) Alan Silvestri

6. The warrior woman Valeria appears in which Conan story written by Robert E. Howard?
   - ☐ a) *The People of the Black Circle*
   - ☐ b) *The Frost-Giant's Daughter*
   - ☐ c) *The Tower of the Elephant*
   - ☐ d) *Red Nails*

7. Which of these is NOT a member of the Hong Kong Cavaliers?
   - ☐ a) Rawhide
   - ☐ b) Zippo
   - ☐ c) Perfect Tommy
   - ☐ d) Big Norse

8. The 1975 film *A Boy and His Dog* is based on a short story by which writer?
   - ☐ a) Alfred Bester
   - ☐ b) Harlan Ellison
   - ☐ c) Philip K. Dick
   - ☐ d) Isaac Asimov

9. Complete this string of numbers "4, 8, 15, 16, 23..."
   - ☐ a) 34
   - ☐ b) 42
   - ☐ c) 54
   - ☐ d) 63

10. Who played the character of Daredevil in the 1989 made-for-television movie, *The Trial of the Incredible Hulk*?
    - ☐ a) Robert Ewing
    - ☐ b) Rex Smith
    - ☐ c) Chuck Colwell
    - ☐ d) Gerald Di Pego

QUIZ 104
GENERAL KNOWLEDGE, MULTIPLE CHOICE

1. Which was the first non-Lucasfilm movie to employ the services of Industrial Light & Magic?
   - ☐ a) *The Dark Crystal*
   - ☐ b) *Dragonslayer*
   - ☐ c) *Innerspace*
   - ☐ d) *Batteries Not Included*

2. What is the Klingon word for "love"?
   - ☐ a) maktag
   - ☐ b) po'tajg
   - ☐ c) gik'tal
   - ☐ d) par'Mach

3. In *The Mists of Avalon*, who is Morgaine's mother?
   - ☐ a) Igraine
   - ☐ b) Morgause
   - ☐ c) Viviane
   - ☐ d) Raven

4. In C. J. Cherryh's *Downbelow Station*, the space station that is the center of the story is in orbit around which planet?
   - ☐ a) Henterra
   - ☐ b) Trace's World
   - ☐ c) Dorrato
   - ☐ d) Pell's World

5. *Ronia, the Robber's Daughter* was originally published in which language?
   - ☐ a) Danish
   - ☐ b) Hungarian
   - ☐ c) Swedish
   - ☐ d) Romanian

6. What is the second book in Gene Wolfe's *The Book of the New Sun* series?

☐ a) *The Shadow of the Torturer*

☐ b) *The Claw of the Conciliator*

☐ c) *The Sword of the Lictor*

☐ d) *The Citadel of the Autarch*

7. What was Morticia Addams' maiden name?

☐ a) Snarl

☐ b) Treed

☐ c) Frump

☐ d) Fester

8. In which year did Robert A. Heinlein die?

☐ a) 1972

☐ b) 1977

☐ c) 1982

☐ d) 1988

9. What was the first expansion for *Magic: The Gathering*?

☐ a) *Legends*

☐ b) *Arabian Nights*

☐ c) *Antiquities*

☐ d) *The Dark*

10. Which actor from *Star Trek: The Original Series* voiced a character in the Disney movie *Atlantis: The Lost Empire*?

☐ a) Leonard Nimoy

☐ b) William Shatner

☐ c) James Doohan

☐ d) Nichelle Nichols

ANSWERS

DIFFICULTY LEVEL: EASY

Quiz 1
1)b 2)a 3)c 4)c 5)d 6)c 7)b 8)a 9)d 10)b

Quiz 2
1)c 2)a 3)c 4)d 5)b 6)a 7)b 8)b 9)c 10)c

Quiz 3
1) False. It was District 12.
2) True.
3) False. It is Peregrin Took.
4) False.
5) True.
6) False. Barsoom was Mars.
7) False. It is green.
8) False. There were several before *Dracula*.
9) False.
10) True.

Quiz 4
1) Tatooine
2) *Terminator 2*
3) "…comes great responsibility."
4) King Arthur
5) *Do Androids Dream of Electric Sheep?* by Philip K. Dick
6) The Hulk (or Dr. Bruce Banner)
7) Third
8) a werewolf
9) Professor X
10) cyberpunk

Quiz 5
1)e 2)i 3)c 4)a 5)j 6)h 7)f 8)d 9)g 10)b

Quiz 6
1)a 2)a 3)c 4)b 5)c 6)c 7)d 8)a 9)d 10)d

Quiz 7
1)b 2)a 3)c 4)b 5)b 6)d 7)c 8)a 9)d 10)b

Quiz 8
1) False.
2) True.
3) True.
4) False. It is half eagle and half lion.
5) True.
6) False. Luke Skywalker appears first.
7) True.
8) False.
9) False. She is an only child.
10) False. It was written by Marion Zimmer Bradley.

Quiz 9
1) *Doctor Who*
2) *Mad Max Beyond Thunderdome*
3) *Discworld*
4) *Hercules: The Legendary Journeys*
5) *The Twilight Zone* (1959)
6) "…in a galaxy far, far away…"
7) *Halo*
8) Mega-City One
9) *Neon Genesis Evangelion*
10) King's Cross

Quiz 10
1)h 2)b 3)j 4)a 5)g 6)c 7)e 8)i 9)f 10)d

Quiz 11
1)d 2)a 3)a 4)d 5)c 6)c 7)c 8)b 9)a 10)c

Quiz 12
1)c 2)b 3)a 4)c 5)b 6)a 7)d 8)b 9)c 10)d

Quiz 13
1) False. His father was Arathorn.
2) True.

3) False. It was written by Edgar Rice Burroughs.
4) False. He is British.
5) True.
6) False. It was made by DreamWorks Animation.
7) False. He is the son of Poseidon.
8) True. (41 novels.)
9) False. He was a Great Old One.
10) False. It is Anne.

Quiz 14
1) The Teenage Mutant Ninja Turtles ("Teenage Mutant Hero Turtles" also accepted).
2) Time And Relative Dimensions In Space
3) Beowulf
4) 1.21 Gigawatts
5) Chaotic Evil
6) *Red Dwarf*
7) Dr. Leonard "Bones" McCoy
8) Kyle Reese
9) Drow (although "Dark Elf" is also acceptable)
10) The Kingpin

Quiz 15
1)d 2)i 3)a 4)j 5)g 6)e 7)b 8)f 9)c 10)h

Quiz 16
1)a 2)b 3)a 4)c 5)d 6)b 7)c 8)d 9)c 10)a

Quiz 17
1)d 2)b 3)a 4)c 5)b 6)a 7)d 8)c 9)a 10)c

Quiz 18
1) False. They are cousins.
2) False.
3) False. It is set in the year 2029.
4) True.
5) True.
6) False. It was an Old English word derived from "orcneas".
7) False. He is a man (or sometimes a giant).
8) False. It was designed by Steve Jackson.
9) True.
10) True.

Quiz 19
1) 451 degrees
2) A Live-Action Role-Playing Game

3) In his house at R'lyeh
4) Michael York
5) *The Prisoner*
6) *Mystery Science Theater 3,000*
7) Icarus
8) A spaceship
9) Batman and Superman
10) 5

Quiz 20
1)f 2)b 3)j 4)i 5)a 6)h 7)c 8)g 9)d 10)e

Quiz 21
1)d 2)b 3)d 4)c 5)b 6)b 7)c 8)b 9)a 10)b

Quiz 22
1)a 2)c 3)d 4)b 5)c 6)c 7)c 8)b 9)d 10)a

Quiz 23
1) True. He wrote 14.
2) False. The print edition of the magazine ceased with number 359.
3) True.
4) True.
5) False.
6) True.
7) False. His middle name is James.
8) True. He played Halvarth.
9) False. William Golding wrote *Lord of the Flies*. William Goldman wrote *The Princess Bride*.
10) False. He died of cancer.

Quiz 24
1) Thor
2) Lynda Carter
3) A virgin
4) Hiro Protagonist
5) *Akira*
6) Mike Mignola
7) Pamela Anderson (or Pamela Anderson-Lee)
8) *World War Z*
9) Robert A. Heinlein
10) White Wolf

Quiz 25
1)h 2)d 3)j 4)b 5)g 6)i 7)f 8)e 9)a 10)c

Quiz 26
1)b 2)c 3)b 4)a 5)d 6)a 7)d 8)a 9)d 10)a

Quiz 27
1)d 2)c 3)a 4)b 5)d 6)a 7)c 8)c 9)b 10)d

Quiz 28
1) True.
2) False.
3) True.
4) False.
5) True.
6) True.
7) False.
8) True. At Boston University.
9) True.
10) True.

Quiz 29
1) Proton torpedo (MG7-A)
2) *The Day the Earth Stood Still*
3) To Hit Armor Class Zero
4) Doctor Who
5) a ring (or The Ring)
6) Man-Thing
7) "An African or European swallow?"
8) *Back to the Future*
9) National Institute of Mental Health
10) seven

Quiz 30
1)h 2)e 3)j 4)c 5)i 6)a 7)g 8)d 9)b 10)f

Quiz 31
1)a 2)b 3)c 4)a 5)d 6)b 7)c 8)b 9)b 10)a

Quiz 32
1)c 2)d 3)b 4)d 5)c 6)a 7)b 8)a 9)d 10)a

Quiz 33
1) True.
2) True.
3) True.
4) False.
5) False. It's in San Francisco, California.
6) False.

7) True.
8) True.
9) False. They are generally good.
10) True.

Quiz 34
1) He has six fingers on his right hand.
2) Mary Jane Watson
3) Whoopi Goldberg
4) Man
5) Orbital Drop Shock Trooper
6) Tanks (specifically hover tanks)
7) *Cowboy Bebop*
8) *Amazing Stories*
9) *Call of Cthulhu*
10) Either. They're both great.

Quiz 35
1)h 2)j 3)b 4)f 5)d 6)a 7)c 8)i 9)e 10)g

ANSWERS

DIFFICULTY LEVEL: MEDIUM

Quiz 36
1)d 2)b 3)a 4)c 5)b 6)b 7)a 8)b 9)b 10)a

Quiz 37
1)a 2)b 3)c 4)d 5)c 6)c 7)a 8)a 9)b 10)b

Quiz 38
1) True.
2) True.
3) False. The robot had no official name and was just called "The Robot."
4) True.
5) False.
6) True. In the 1978 *Star Wars Holiday Special*.
7) False. It is a Galaxy-class starship.
8) True. The character is either called "The Hatter" or "Hatta."
9) True.
10) False.

Quiz 39
1) 1974
2) White, Black, Red, Green, Blue
3) Sarlacc
4) Bill Finger and Bob Kane
5) Karl Urban
6) Boris Karloff
7) Martian Manhunter
8) Oz
9) Wesley Snipes
10) Massively Multiplayer Online Role-Playing Game

Quiz 40

1)g 2)a 3)j 4)e 5)h 6)b 7)d 8)i 9)c 10)f

Quiz 41

1)d 2)b 3)c 4)d 5)d 6)b 7)d 8)b 9)b 10)d

Quiz 42

1)b 2)b 3)d 4)b 5)a 6)c 7)a 8)d 9)b 10)b

Quiz 43

1) False. He loses his right hand.
2) True. He was Prince Abdullah when he briefly appeared in the episode "Investigations".
3) False. He first appeared in 1963.
4) True.
5) True.
6) False. It only ran for a single season on Spike TV.
7) False. He also appears in *The Mysterious Island*.
8) True.
9) False. It made it to third behind *Avatar* and *Titanic*.
10) True. The Doctor in *Star Trek: Voyager* and Richard Woolsey in all three *Stargate* shows.

Quiz 44

1) wings
2) Dave Arneson
3) Tribbles
4) *The Twilight Zone*
5) two: *Swamp Thing* and *The Return of Swamp Thing*
6) William Shatner
7) Manu Bennett
8) sequel
9) Olaf Stapledon
10) *The Quickening*

Quiz 45

1)h 2)c 3)j 4)i 5)a 6)f 7)g 8)d 9)e 10)b

Quiz 46

1)b 2)c 3)c 4)b 5)a 6)d 7)a 8)c 9)d 10)a

Quiz 47

1)b 2)b 3)a 4)c 5)d 6)c 7)c 8)c 9)a 10)d

Quiz 48

1) False. He was created by Len Wein and Bernie Wrightson.
2) True. He plays the grandfather.
3) False.

4) True.

5) False. It was 1923.

6) False.

7) True. He wrote 14 episodes.

8) True. Although his kingdom is small, dull, and dreary.

9) True.

10) True.

Quiz 49

1) *The Modern Prometheus*

2) George Lucas

3) Prince Imrahil of Dol Amroth

4) *Space Battleship Yamato*

5) John Sheridan

6) *Eaters of the Dead* by Michael Crichton

7) Hellboy

8) Echo Base

9) vibranium

10) a jackrabbit with antlers

Quiz 50

1)f 2)h 3)j 4)d 5)i 6)a 7)b 8)e 9)g 10)c

Quiz 51

1)b 2)d 3)d 4)d 5)c 6)d 7)b 8)a 9)b 10)c

Quiz 52

1)a 2)c 3)d 4)b 5)b 6)d 7)b 8)c 9)a 10)c

Quiz 53

1) False. The book was published in 1887; Haggard died in 1925.

2) True. It ran for one season in 2007.

3) True. He was the 18th Baron of Dunsany.

4) True.

5) False. It is based on a short film called *La Jetée*.

6) True. He played Professor Filius Flitwick and Griphook the Goblin (in the last two films in the series).

7) False. That honor belongs to *The Sword of Shannara* by Terry Brooks in 1977.

8) False. It is half elf and half spider.

9) True.

10) True.

Quiz 54

1) *Starship Troopers*

2) Image Comics

3) Rodents Of Unusual Size

4) *Xena: Warrior Princess* (134 episodes; there were 111 episodes of *Hercules: The Legendary Journeys*).

5) Bill(y) Mumy who played Will Robinson in *Lost in Space* and Lennier in *Babylon 5*.

6) "...No evil shall escape my sight."

7) Will Eisner

8) 3

9) Richard Garfield

10) *Weird Tales* (1923)

Quiz 55
1)f 2)h 3)a 4)g 5)j 6)b 7)c 8)d 9)e 10)i

Quiz 56
1)b 2)c 3)d 4)a 5)c 6)c 7)a 8)d 9)b 10)d

Quiz 57
1)b 2)b 3)d 4)d 5)c 6)c 7)a 8)c 9)b 10)a

Quiz 58
1) True. It ran for two seasons.
2) True.
3) False. It was entitled *Doctor Sleep*.
4) True.
5) True.
6) False. Worldwide sales are close to half a billion.
7) True.
8) False.
9) True.
10) False.

Quiz 59
1) 6: d4, d6, d8, d10, d12, d20
2) *A Canticle For Leibowitz*
3) Karl Urban
4) *Caprica*
5) *Y: The Last Man*
6) Latveria
7) Treebeard
8) Luke Cage, Power Man
9) *A Dream of Spring*
10) Ouroboros

Quiz 60
1)b 2)f 3)i 4)c 5)a 6)e 7)h 8)j 9)g 10)d

Quiz 61

1)b 2)c 3)c 4)a 5)a 6)c 7)a 8)d 9)c 10)d

Quiz 62

1)d 2)c 3)a 4)c 5)b 6)b 7)c 8)b 9)d 10)d

Quiz 63

1) True. In 1986 and 1987 respectively.
2) True. It ran for 14 episodes in 1977–78.
3) False. Only the first season was filmed in black and white.
4) True.
5) False.
6) True. As the voice of the starliner *Axiom*'s computer.
7) True.
8) False.
9) False. The character was played by Bob Peck.
10) True.

Quiz 64

1) The Vorpal Blade
2) Mance Rayder
3) *Eragon*
4) The Midgard Serpent (or Jörmungardr)
5) Vala Mal Doran
6) *Halo*
7) James Howlett
8) *The Fifth Element*
9) *The Legend of Zelda*
10) Paul Bettany

Quiz 65

1)c 2)h 3)j 4)a 5)f 6)b 7)i 8)d 9)g 10)e

ANSWERS

DIFFICULTY LEVEL: HARD

Quiz 66
1)d 2)c 3)b 4)d 5)c 6)c 7)b 8)d 9)d 10)c

Quiz 67
1)c 2)d 3)a 4)b 5)b 6)d 7)b 8)a 9)d 10)b

Quiz 68
1) True.
2) True. Arnold Schwarzenegger (California) and Jesse Ventura (Minnesota).
3) True.
4) False. He served in the Confederate Army.
5) True. *Total Recall 2070* ran for a single series in 1999.
6) True.
7) False.
8) True.
9) False. It was written by A. Merritt.
10) False. It is generally considered to be in the 1960s.

Quiz 69
1) Michael Crichton
2) Roger Delgado
3) *Space Battleship Yamato*
4) Virgil
5) *The X-Files*
6) Thulsa Doom
7) Gotham City (Arkham, Massachusetts is also acceptable).
8) Bruce Campbell
9) *Planetary*
10) *The Hunger Games*

Quiz 70

1)f 2)j 3)h 4)a 5)c 6)i 7)b 8)d 9)g 10)e

Quiz 71

1)c 2)a 3)c 4)a 5)a 6)b 7)b 8)b 9)c 10)d

Quiz 72

1)c 2)d 3)c 4)b 5)d 6)b 7)b 8)a 9)c 10)b

Quiz 73

1) False. David Carson directed *Star Trek: Generations*. Jonathan Frakes made his debut on the next movie in the series, *Star Trek: First Contact*.
2) False. That was a different sword, Excalibur was a gift from the Lady of the Lake.
3) True.
4) False. He played Harvey Dent. Pat Hingle played Commissioner Gordon.
5) True. They came from the planet Mor-Tax.
6) True.
7) False. The character's name is Thursday Next.
8) True.
9) True.
10) False.

Quiz 74

1) *Ewoks*
2) mango juice (from the theme song to *Red Dwarf*)
3) Bending
4) The blood of a Christian man
5) Miles Morales
6) Kaywinnet Lee Frye
7) *Dungeon*
8) Bureau for Paranormal Research and Defense
9) Green Arrow (1941). Hawkeye was created in 1964.
10) *Stargate: SG-1*

Quiz 75

1)g 2)b 3)i 4)f 5)e 6)a 7)h 8)j 9)d 10)c

Quiz 76

1)c 2)d 3)b 4)b 5)c 6)b 7)a 8)a 9)d 10)b

Quiz 77

1)c 2)d 3)a 4)a 5)d 6)c 7)d 8)b 9)a 10)b

Quiz 78

1) True.

2) True.
3) False. He had a Ph.D. in Chemical Engineering.
4) True.
5) False. He played the Reman Viceroy in *Star Trek: Nemesis*.
6) True.
7) True.
8) False.
9) False. It did win four, but not the award for Best Picture.
10) False.

Quiz 79
1) Unseen University
2) Alfred Bester
3) *Legend*
4) Peter Cushing
5) John Rhys-Davies
6) Loki
7) Theseus
8) Harlan Ellison
9) id Software
10) gold farming

Quiz 80
1)c 2)f 3)j 4)i 5)e 6)a 7)g 8)b 9)h 10)d

Quiz 81
1)b 2)a 3)d 4)b 5)b 6)c 7)c 8)a 9)b 10)c

Quiz 82
1)d 2)a 3)c 4)d 5)a 6)c 7)b 8)c 9)d 10)b

Quiz 83
1) False. It is called *Transmetropolitan*.
2) False. He failed once.
3) False. The role was played by Alicia Silverstone.
4) True.
5) True.
6) True.
7) False. The character has no name.
8) False. It was published in 1997.
9) True.
10) False. It was around 12 years.

Quiz 84
1) Obsidian
2) Jeff Smith

3) Gary Gygax

4) *Neuromancer* by William Gibson

5) Karl Urban

6) Frank Oz

7) *The Sarah Jane Adventures*

8) Visitors or Victory (either answer is acceptable)

9) Coke (more specifically New Coke)

10) Dry-roasted peanuts

Quiz 85

1)d 2)i 3)b 4)h 5)f 6)a 7)c 8)j 9)e 10)g

Quiz 86

1)a 2)b 3)d 4)b 5)b 6)a 7)a 8)a 9)a 10)b

Quiz 87

1)d 2)b 3)c 4)d 5)d 6)c 7)a 8)b 9)c 10)d

Quiz 88

1) True.

2) False. He first appeared in a comic called *Albedo Anthropomorphics*.

3) False. He plays Gawain.

4) True.

5) True.

6) True.

7) False. It was mainly filmed in England and Ireland.

8) True. John DiMaggio.

9) True.

10) True.

Quiz 89

1) Stanley Martin Lieber

2) *Time Bandits*

3) "…The Shadow knows!"

4) Mark Steven Johnson

5) Philip José Farmer

6) Glyphs

7) Stephen King

8) David Eddings

9) *Buffy the Vampire Slayer*

10) House Tully

Quiz 90

1)f 2)i 3)b 4)a 5)j 6)d 7)e 8)c 9)h 10)g

Quiz 91

1)c 2)d 3)a 4)b 5)d 6)b 7)a 8)d 9)c 10)c

Quiz 92

1)c 2)c 3)b 4)a 5)a 6)b 7)d 8)d 9)c 10)a

Quiz 93

1) False. The *Lensman* series finished second to the *Foundation* trilogy by Isaac Asimov.
2) False.
3) False. There were 14 episodes.
4) True.
5) True.
6) True.
7) False. It is *Mobile Armored Riot Police*.
8) True. *The Armageddon Rag*.
9) True.
10) False.

Quiz 94

1) 1997
2) Generic Universal RolePlaying System
3) *Ewoks: The Battle for Endor*
4) Kristy Swanson
5) Tokyo
6) The Dwarves
7) Caliber Comics
8) a dragon
9) Anne McCaffrey
10) Japanimation

Quiz 95

1)f 2)i 3)e 4)j 5)c 6)b 7)a 8)h 9)d 10)g

Quiz 96

1)c 2)d 3)c 4)d 5)c 6)a 7)a 8)b 9)a 10)d

Quiz 97

1)c 2)a 3)d 4)b 5)d 6)b 7)d 8)c 9)a 10)b

Quiz 98

1) True.
2) True. David Webb Peoples.
3) True. He played the Romulan Commander Tomalak.
4) False.
5) False. Hamill and Spiner have; Anderson has not.
6) True.

7) True. *Der Orchideengarten*, which ran from 1919–21.

8) False. It is the story of H. G. Wells and his time machine.

9) True. "The Vengeance of Nitocris."

10) False. It relocated to Ireland.

Quiz 99
1) *Return of the Jedi*
2) Stargate
3) Salusa Secundus
4) Chicken Legs
5) Daleks
6) Jean-Luc Godard
7) *Hardware*
8) Seabury Quinn
9) Ray Parker, Jr.
10) *In the Name of the King*

Quiz 100
1)h 2)d 3)j 4)g 5)i 6)f 7)a 8)e 9)b 10)c

Quiz 101
1)b 2)c 3)a 4)d 5)a 6)d 7)c 8)d 9)d 10)a

Quiz 102
1)b 2)a 3)b 4)d 5)c 6)b 7)c 8)a 9)c 10)d

Quiz 103
1)d 2)a 3)b 4)b 5)c 6)d 7)b 8)b 9)b 10)b

Quiz 104
1)b 2)d 3)a 4)d 5)c 6)b 7)c 8)d 9)b 10)a

AUTHOR/QUIZMASTER

Joseph A. McCullough is the author of several non-fiction books including *A Pocket History of Ireland*, *Zombies: A Hunter's Guide*, and *Dragonslayers: From Beowulf to St. George*. In addition, his fantasy short stories have appeared in various books and magazines such as *Black Gate*, *Lords of Swords*, and *Adventure Mystery Tales*. He is also the creator of the wargame *Frostgrave: Fantasy Wargames in the Frozen City*, and co-wrote *The Grey Mountains*, a supplement for the Middle-Earth Role-Playing game. His continued ramblings can be read at: http://therenaissancetroll.blogspot.co.uk

ILLUSTRATOR

Miguel Coimbra is a self-taught freelance artist, currently living near Lyon, France. He has been working in the industry for 10 years, first as a graphic designer, then as a concept artist for video games. He is also well-known in the board game industry, having worked on many award-winning titles like *Smallworld* and *7 Wonders*. His favorite themes are fantasy and mythology. You can find more of his work at www.miguelcoimbra.com